Islamic Banking and Finance

This book discusses the nature and theories which govern systems of Islamic finance including its most distinctive features and its relationship with conventional financial institutions.

It explores the nature and role of money in modern economies and elaborates on the process of credit deposit creation, trade cycles and instruments for the creation of value in financial markets through the perspectives of Islamic finance. The author explains its characteristics, especially the rationale for the lack of interest-based financial activities. He examines the intrinsic ethical and humanistic frameworks that govern financial theories and practices and the models for the creation of value, risk-sharing and socially responsible investing, as well as the governance and regulation that these systems follow. The author also does a comparative assessment of conventional financial systems with Islamic finance with relevant examples, assesses the performance of Islamic systems and examines existing and expanding markets for Islamic finance.

Lucid and cogent, this book is useful for scholars and researchers of Islamic finance, Islamic studies, economics, banking and finance in general.

Zubair Hasan is an acclaimed economist and author. He taught at the University of Delhi and the International Islamic University of Malaysia. He has published numerous articles, commentaries and book reviews in academic journals of repute on topics in economics and finance. In recognition of his numerous contributions, he was awarded the prestigious Islamic Development Bank Prize in Islamic Economics in 2009.

Islamic Banking and Finance

Second Edition

Zubair Hasan

LONDON AND NEW YORK

Second edition published 2023
by Routledge
4 Park Square, Milton Park, Abingdon, Oxon, OX14 4RN

and by Routledge
605 Third Avenue, New York, NY 10158

Routledge is an imprint of the Taylor & Francis Group, an informa business

© 2023 Zubair Hasan

The right of Zubair Hasan to be identified as author of this work has been asserted in accordance with sections 77 and 78 of the Copyright, Designs and Patents Act 1988.

All rights reserved. No part of this book may be reprinted or reproduced or utilised in any form or by any electronic, mechanical, or other means, now known or hereafter invented, including photocopying and recording, or in any information storage or retrieval system, without permission in writing from the publishers.

Trademark notice: Product or corporate names may be trademarks or registered trademarks, and are used only for identification and explanation without intent to infringe.

First edition published by Oxford University Press 2014

British Library Cataloguing-in-Publication Data
A catalogue record for this book is available from the British Library

ISBN: 978-1-032-36064-5 (hbk)
ISBN: 978-1-032-43363-9 (pbk)
ISBN: 978-1-003-36697-3 (ebk)

DOI: 10.4324/9781003366973

Typeset in Sabon
by SPi Technologies India Pvt Ltd (Straive)

Contents

List of figures	vi
List of tables	viii
Preface to the second edition	ix
Glossary	xii

1	Introduction to Islamic finance	1
2	Value of money, trade cycles and social consequences	10
3	Islamic finance: The basics	21
4	Contracts and instruments	35
5	Financing consumer durables	46
6	Islamic financial markets character and instruments	59
7	Investment sukuk: Islamic bonds	75
8	Risk and risk management	91
9	Islam and insurance (takaful)	109
10	Law regulation and governance	124

Appendix	144
Bibliography	149
Index	152

Figures

1.1	Volume of credit generated (million dollars)	2
1.2	Time value of money in Islamic sale	5
2.1	Phases of a trade cycle	12
2.2	Real and money flows in a two-sector, closed economy	13
2.3	Seasonal variations	14
2.4	Profit-sharing ratio in a state of equilibrium in an Islamic economy	15
3.1	Fertility rates	23
3.2	Growth of Islamic financial assets (trillion US dollars)	24
3.3	Islamic finance: The nominal-real circuitry	30
3.4	The 2007 turmoil and Islamic finance	32
4.1	Process of profit sharing under the mixed-mudarabah system	40
4.2	PSR determination for the bank	41
5.1	Compounding enters all home financing where the EMIs are uniform	51
5.2	ZDBM structure – contracts, parties, and their interconnections	54
5.3	Rate of ownership transfer to the customer is less than pro rata in the MMP	55
6.1	Capital Market Mediation	61
6.2	*Salam* and parallel *salam* operations	68
6.3	Istisna' in operation	69
6.4	The BBA structure	71
6.5	The two uses of tawaruq	72
7.1	General structure of mudarabah-based sukuk	80
7.2	Operational structure of musharakah sukuk	81
7.3	Common structure of ijara sukuk	83
7.4	Structure of murabahah sukuk	84
7.5	The use of murabahah sukuk in Kazakhstan	85
7.6	General structure of slum	85
7.7	Structure and contract sequence of istasna sukuk	86
7.8	Istasna sukuk in operation	87

8.1	Risk aversion	92
8.2	The risk wheel	100
8.3	Risk management cycle	102
9.1	Mudarabah model in family takaful	118
9.2	Operational framework in waqf takaful	119

Tables

1.1	The credit creation process	2
3.1	Muslim versus world population growth	24
5.1	Worksheet the parties have based on the illustration data	50
5.2	Waiver of compounding must make EMIs unequal	52
5.3	Working of the diminishing balance model	53
5.4	ZDBM and MMP: Comparative position (amount $)	54
5.5	Ownership transfer versus payment rate	55
8.1	Swap operation illustration	106

Preface to the second edition

Oxford University Press, Malaysia, published this work as a textbook under the title *Islamic Banking and Finance – An Integrative Approach*, in 2014. I think the book has since served university students well across countries. However, much has changed in the theory and practice of Islamic finance over time and space. Its canvass has widened beyond expectations. It has emerged as a challenger to interest-based finance as a turmoil-free alternative. The content and the speed of change demanded a revision of the work.

The revision frees the work of its textbook confines. Learning outcomes, marginal notes, exercises. Boxes case studies, test questions, and whatnot have all been dropped. Two of the chapters have also been excluded. The language, diagrams and material sequencing have been improved, dead wood removed and the latest developments and information included.

Despite these changes, I did not want to lose sight of the student community for whom I worked for 58 long years with affection and earnestness. My continuing concern for them is reflected in the chapter structuring of the book.

After the title, each chapter has a brief table of contents and a brief summary at the end. The book also has a glossary. Additionally, the language, diagrams and material sequencing have been updated, dead wood has been removed and recent developments and information have been included. The bibliography contains scholarly writings related to the content of the chapters.

Chapter 1, "Introduction to Islamic Finance," recognizes the relationship between conventional and Islamic finance via the monetary link. It explains the nature and role of money in modern economies, elaborates on the process of credit deposit creation and examines the importance of finance in running an economy. It explains the characteristics of Islamic finance, especially the rationale for banning interest. It closes with a brief narration of the historical evolution of Islamic finance.

Chapter 2, "Value of Money, Trade Cycles and Social Consequences", explains the nature of booms and depressions occurring in modern economies and their impact on the circular monetary and real flows relationship. It examines their social consequences, especially from the angle of

x Preface to the second edition

distributive justice. It looks at the related public policies from an Islamic perspective.

Chapter 3, "Islamic Finance: The Basics," explains the convergence of Islamic finance to the conventional and its consequences. It talks about the internationalization of Islamic finance and its performance vis-à-vis the conventional, especially during the 2007 turmoil. It examines the desired possibility of Gold Dinar.

Chapter 4, "Contracts and Instruments," lists and explains the Islamic maxims relating to finance, participatory modes of finance, the determination of sharing ratios and the impact of funds' demand and supply on them in a macro-setting. It highlights a temporal division of the modes.

Chapter 5, "Financing Consumer Durables," using home financing as an illustration the treatment, shows that no method of paying uniform installments equated monthly installment (EMIs) can be free of compounding the return on capital, or can compounding be isolated and paid back by making installments unequal. Since Islamic banks have been using uniform installment payments, consumer durables like home financing are not Shari'ah compliant. It is un-Islamic also for the reason that the ownership transfer to the buyer in the breach of the contract is adverse. A rule-bound alternative is presented.

Chapter 6, "Islamic Financial Markets," deals with money and capital markets and their operations. It explains the direct and indirect modes, contracts and mode combinations, including murbahah, musharikah, ijara, salam, BBA, tawaruq, qard hasan.

Chapter 7, "Investment Sukuk: Islamic Bonds," explains the meaning, structuring and significance of sukuk in Islamic finance. The chapter also examines sukuk markets expansion and problems.

Chapter 8, Risk and Risk Management," explains the concept of risk and its Islamic view and distinguishes between the sharing of risk and its transfer. The types of risks are indicated, and the methods to manage them are explained.

Chapter 9, "Islamic and Insurance (Takaful)," explains the concept of insurance and its basic principles and elaborates on the Islamic view of insurance, its types and operations including retakaful. Some insurance related concepts like insurable interest, good faith and indemnity are also discussed.

Chapter 10, "Law, Regulation and Governance," is a lengthy chapter that discusses diverse theories and practices of Islamic finance across countries. It examines the interface issues between common law, civil law and the Shari'ah. Liquidity-profit trade-off issues and solutions are examined. Various regulatory complexities are discussed. Basel Accords and Islamic finance standard fixing are analyzed and problems and challenges of governance examined.

The revision and updating have been so thorough, that what we now have is virtually a new book.

Zubair Hasan
Professor Emeritus, INCEIF 49, Zakir Bagh,
New Delhi – 25 September 2021
www.zubairhasan.in

Glossary

AAOIFI This is the abbreviation of the Accounting and Auditing Organization for Islamic Financial Institutions, which is based in Bahrain. Established on 27 March 1991, the organization works toward the achievement the following objectives:

- To conduct and support research
- To develop accounting and auditing concepts and standards relevant to Islamic financial institutions
- To disseminate these concepts and standards through training seminars and the publication of periodicals and newsletters
- To review and amend periodically the existing accounting and auditing standards

Bai al dayn The Arabic term is translated as the sale of a debt that results from the transactions relating to the trade of goods and services in the form of payment or delivery of deferred goods. In Malaysia, they have a mixed opinion about debt: debt has to come from an allowable Islamic contract, as defined by the *Shari'ah* Advisory Council of the Security Commission. Until 2007, the most popular *sukuk* issued in the country were BBA-based debt (*dayn*) instruments.

Basel Pillars There are three basics relating to capital that constitute the core of Basel Accords They are known as the Basel Pillars. They were part of Basel I in 1988 and were retained in subsequent Accords, but they have been improved by expanding and tightening them with every new Accord

Benefit provisions Benefits provision refers to the compensations that are available under family *takaful* on (i) the death of the policyholder, (ii) any disability the policyholder may suffer and (iii) the maturing of the policy.

Bonds Bonds are debt certificates embodying capital investment. They are classified as fixed-return securities. With a fixed rate of return (interest) and the return of the principal sum guaranteed, the traditional bond violates the Islamic norm that prohibits earning money from *riba*.

Business cycles A business cycle is a sequence of inflation peak – recession – depression bottom or trough – recover – inflation. Peaks are narrow with sharp turns while bottoms are broader and painful. There are numerous theories to explain cycles – from sunspots to human psychology.

Capital adequacy ratio (CAR) This measures the asset ability of a bank to meet its long-term liabilities on time and also to cover other risks, such as credit risk or operational risk. Put simply, it is an assessment of whether a bank has assets sufficient to cushion potential losses and can protect its depositors and other lenders. Banking regulators in most countries define and monitor CAR to protect depositors, thereby maintaining confidence in the banking system. CAR equals equity over assets.

Commodity *murabahah* In general, some real commodity must be at the root of all *urabahah* contracts, but commodity *murabahah* has of late emerged as a term in its own right. The term has become popular in the market as implying a contract of *bai-al-tawarruq* discussed in the text. It is a contract that permits a person to buy an asset from a seller under deferred payment, which the person sells subsequently to a third party in order to obtain cash. The transaction is called *tawarruq* because the intention of the buyer is not to benefit from the physical use of the asset but to obtain liquidity to overcome a temporary cash shortage.

Commodity *murabahah/tawarruq* Like other Islamic finance instruments, commodity *murabahah* transactions cannot exist without an underlying commodity (asset). Why, then, attach a commodity explicitly to this instrument? The reason is that in 2007, Bank Negara in Malaysia launched what is known as the Commodity *Murabahah* Programme as a part of its initiative to support the development of Islamic finance. The program facilitates inter-bank liquidity management and investment.

Common law The body of customary law based on judicial decisions and embodied in reports of decided cases. It has been administered by the common law courts of England since the Middle Ages. From it has evolved the type of legal system now found also in the United States and in most of the member states of the Commonwealth. In this sense, common law stands in contrast to the legal system derived from civil law, which is now widespread across countries. Even today, if a case remains disputed in the civil courts, it can be taken to the common law court and its decision would prevail as the last word. Customary law, known as *urf*, is well recognized in Islamic heritage.

Constructive ownership An agent holding the assets of a principal with his permission with the authority granted to manage them as if the owner.

Contractual risk transfer Risk can be transferred to another entity through a contract or an agreement. This involves the transfer of legal liability for performing an activity and bearing the financial losses that may follow in its wake.

xiv Glossary

Deflation It is a situation where output, incomes, employment, savings and investments chase one another in a downward spiral.

Displaced commercial risk This risk is unique to participatory finance in Islamic banking. In a pure *mudarabah* investment, the financing of a project is undertaken by the bank on the stipulation that the profit will be shared with the depositors, but the depositors alone will bear the risk of a loss. However, if the loss is in fact suffered, the bank does not pass it all to the depositors. In order to maintain their confidence and retain them as customers, the bank will also bear a part of the loss. This is called 'displaced commercial risk,' and capital cover for it is included in the calculation of the CAR.

Ethical investments Investment in industries or activities that are considered desirable by social secular norms or by the Islamic faith.

Financial insurance A re-insurance scheme with a view toward spreading risk, usually in the case of life insurance. This helps the operator to grow in the market.

Gharar Justice and fair play are the foundation stones of all contractual relationships in Islam: parties to a transaction must avoid as far as possible causing harm to each other. Any chance of financial injury to any of the parties due to the *indeterminacy* of the subject matter, modes of operation or interpretation of clauses is not permitted. Sales of fruits on trees, standing crops, unborn animals and goods on high seas are restricted in Islam to minimize loss due to gharar.

Group family *takaful* The policy covers education, health care and other specifications, i.e. clauses agreed upon for all the group members.

Hired and un-hired factors The un-hired factor, in modern parlance, is the entrepreneur who guarantees the payment of preset compensation to hired factors for their contribution to his productive effort. Entrepreneurs must preferably own capital or must at least have control of (liquid) resources to meet their contractual obligations for paying the hired factors' wages, rent and interest, and to hold minimal inventories to ensure unhindered, smooth production. The entrepreneur of today is the Islamic *mudarib* of yesterday. The affinity between capitalism and Islam on this point is close and vivid. It brings the need for, and methods of, risk management in Islam and capitalism closer.

Ijarah The leasing or selling of the right to use an asset according to the terms of the rental contract. The ownership of the asset is not transferred to the lease; only the usufruct of the asset, say a house, is sold.

Indemnity Guaranteed protection against financial loss caused by an event that is covered by the policy, such as fire, flood, theft or accidents.

Inflation When incomes are expanding faster than the production of real goods and services in an economy, inflation is taking place; prices tend to rise continually.

Glossary xv

Insurable interest This is an insurance principle that a policy is not enforceable unless its beneficiary stands to suffer a direct financial loss if the insured event does take place.

Insurance pricing Generally, the price determination process for insurance products (policies) involves the drawing up of a plan consisting of the relevant assumptions, specifying the products, the state of competition in the market and expected financial outcomes.

Ju'alah Defined in the Iranian usury-free banking law of 1983, it authorizes banks to provide various types of services for a fee or commission. The nature, description of the service and the price charged must be candidly stated in the contract. *Ju'alah* may operate both ways: the bank may employ an outside agency to obtain some services that the banks may want to outsource for a payment.

Maturity mismatch This refers to the mismatch between liability payments and assets income caused by the inability to liquidate the assets in time as the policies mature. Such a mismatch may threaten the very existence of an insurance company.

Mudarabah A pre-Islamic form of business organization, presumably the forerunner of the modern partnership businesses in some measure. It is a sort of participatory business more suitable for project financing. Here, a person with money invests a sum in a business with a person (the entrepreneur) who proposes the business venture in return for receiving an agreed share of the profit. In a pure *mudarabah* model, the entrepreneur is an empty-handed person; in the case of a loss, the entrepreneur alone suffers. The reputation of the entrepreneur is tarnished. The capital providers supply the capital investment. The capital providers bear the loss of the capital they contributed. If there is profit, it will be shared according to a previously agreed-upon ratio.

Musharakah A partnership contract in which all participants contribute to the business. Providers of capital are entitled to participate in the management of the business but do not have to exercise this right if they choose not to. The profit is distributed among the partners in pre-agreed ratios, but the losses, if any, are to be shared in their capital contribution ratios.

Options An option is a derivative instrument that gives its holder, for the price he/she pays, the right to force or not to force the counterparty to meet its obligation under the contract. Options are used to hedge risks that could possibly be caused by adverse movements, say, in commodity prices, rates of return or currency exchange rates.

Pro rata transfer of ownership At each time point in the contract, the ratio of property ownership transfer to the buyer is the same as the proportion of the total amount due he has paid.

Proximate clause This is a *takaful* principle that makes the operator liable only for the loss resulting from the cause proximate (nearest) to the one insured against. Loss caused by an unexpected, remote or uninsured cause is not compensated. The principle has significant legal implications.

Risk and uncertainty Economic theory has invariably sought the source of profit (loss) in what makes competition depart from the ideal, profitless exchange. Frank H. Knight saw it in the dynamic change that gives rise to uncertainty about the future course of events and makes predictions difficult. But he divided uncertainty into measurable and unmeasurable parts. Measurable uncertainty can be insured against; it can be met at a cost (premium) and cannot give rise to economic profit. The part of uncertainty that cannot be measured is *true* uncertainty, which breeds risk. Society offers profit as the reward for those who can successfully manage this uncertainty to their advantage. Uncertainty divides society into those who prefer risk-taking in the hope of big rewards and those who are more cautious and prefer to have guaranteed, fixed incomes to avoid income uncertainty.

Salam/Salaf The term includes transactions embodying forward sales for providing working capital to businesses. Banks in Iran are authorized to purchase the future output of firms by paying the price in advance. The confiscation of the product in terms of quality and measurement must be clarified at the time of the contract, and the price should not exceed the prevalent market charge. Banks are not allowed to sell contracted goods until they obtain their physical possession. The time dimension of a *salaf* transaction cannot normally exceed a production cycle or a year, whichever is shorter.

Special purpose vehicle (SPV) AAIOFI thought the legal creation of a SPV was advisable for the smooth issuance of *sukuk*. SPV acquires assets with the issuance proceeds it obtains from the subscribers and holds it as a trustee on their behalf. It helps ease certain legal rigidities relating to asset ownership in *sukuk* transactions.

Speculation Taking a chance for a gain at the cost of possible loss. Betting or trading in futures is an example. Islam prohibits such chance games.

Sukuk for agriculture AAOIFI has taken an expedient, temporal and spatial view in designing its financing standards. Thus, to accommodate the financial needs of the agricultural sector, it has standardized *muzaarah* (sharecropping) certificates, *musaqah* (irrigation) certificates and *mugharasah* (agricultural) certificates.

Swaps A derivative contract between two parties, say A and B, which allows them to exchange the cash flows of their investments. They use notional capital investment. Swaps are most popular in interest rate hedging.

Trust Laws across countries contain the concept of trust. The SPV, the central piece in *sukuk* issuance, acts as a trustee for the certificate holders. It enables them to own an interest in *sukuk* assets. In conventional securitization, an originator – the one who requires finance – creates a trust to hold the legal title of an asset, of which the SPV is the beneficiary. This conventional trust framework is now being used in the issuance of *sukuk*.

Value of money What packet of goods and services a unit of money can purchase at a time and place is the measure of its value. Thus, the value of money is inverse to the price level. Stability in the value of money is essential for economic and social progress.

Chapter 1

Introduction to Islamic finance

Learning outcomes:

Studying this chapter will enable you to understand:

- Significance of money in modern economies
- Finance and creation of wealth
- The Islamic perspectives on financing
- The definitional points of Islamic finance
- The operational framework for Islamic finance
- The current status and position of Islamic finance

1.1 Money and finance

Money is the most liquid form of wealth in the sense that it can readily be converted into other assets. This sets the ease and speed with which an asset could be converted into cash as a measure of its liquidity. Financial institutions like banks earn their income mostly by using the money (M) of others – i.e., of their depositors. A fraction of all deposits, say F = 5%, each bank has to keep with the central bank of the country; the remaining can be used for advancing credit. Normally only a fraction of the deposits, say R = 10%, are withdrawn daily by the depositors of a bank, thus keeping most in cash, banks lend to short-term borrowers as loans, crediting their accounts and earning money. Thus, loans create deposits. The process has a snowballing effect. The credit multiplier, M = 1/R (1–F). For example, in our case,

$$M = 1 / 0.1(1 - 0.05) \text{ or } 9.5.$$

This means that if the bank has \$50 million cash, it can expand credit up to 50 × 9.5 = \$ 475 m. It would generate 104 layers of credit, as shown in Table 1.1 and Figure 1.1.

DOI: 10.4324/9781003366973-1

2 Introduction to Islamic finance

Table 1.1 The credit creation process

Row No.	1	2	3	4	5
Credit creation (m. $)	42.75	38.570	34.63	31.16	28.1
Row No.	100	101	102	103	104
Credit creation (m. $)	0.001	0.001	0.001	0.001	0

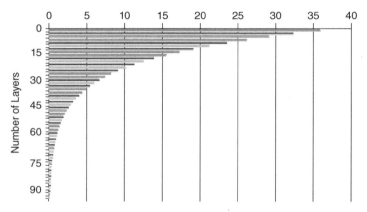

Figure 1.1 Volume of credit generated (million dollars).[1]

To keep their assets liquid is their first principle of business. There has to be a sagacious tradeoff between profit and liquidity. Assets in the balance sheet of a bank are arranged from the bottom with reference to the degree of their liquidity, with cash at the top down to buildings at the bottom, the reverse of a manufacturing firm. Liquidity provides a sort of insurance cover to capital shrinkage. Liquidity concerns are central to modern finance.

Finance refers to providing money for individuals, their groups, or enterprises in the private or public sectors of an economy through institutional or departmental arrangements for general or specified purposes. The ever-expanding paraphernalia of its systems within and across national borders has given rise to financial economics that analyzes the use and distribution of monetary resources in market economies. Even studying the influence of psychological factors on financial behavior patterns has assumed the status of a distinct subject.

1.2 Finance and wealth creation

Finance is the lifeblood of modern economies. It lubricates the wheels of trade, industry and commerce for wealth creation and running the public administration. Finance helps direct resources to various uses; it shapes the volume and distribution of wealth within nations and globally. Over time, pure financial transactions have far outstripped those of real goods and services. More than a trillion US dollars circulate every 24 hours in the foreign exchange markets alone of the world. The dominance of finance over the real sectors has subjugated economic factors in pricing to political manipulations via international corporations, cartels and institutions leading to recurring crises. The chaotic tendency of the financial markets has called for controls and brought in the local central banking regulations supplemented recently with the international Basel Accords. Some of the reasons for the controls, managerial in nature, are as follows:

1   Businesses handle enormous amounts of money every day. This money has to be used further to pay bills, delegate funds, and invest in multiple engagements. Efficiently managing the in and out flows of money in an organization efficiently becomes important.
2   Businesses must minimize their costs for given tasks. Accounting for costs is essential. Firms must avoid overcapitalization of their business but also have sufficient funds to deal with emergency situations.
3   Organizations work to grow and scale up their businesses. Sound financial planning helps an organization meet its expansion goals and face crises with confidence.
4   Governments have no money of their own; they collect it from people and spend it for their cause. They are prone to misuse it or use it wastefully. Parliamentary or other constitutional institutions keep surveillance on the budgetary processes, albeit failures are not uncommon.

1.3 Islam and finance

In this section, we confine our discussion to explaining the nature and significance of Islamic finance. Our approach is integrative. For in the entire Muslim world, Islamic finance is operating along with the mainstream, not in isolation. Their financial systems are dualistic. We shall explain the nature and significance of Islamic finance with this dualistic perspective.

Academics, practitioners and system regulators often begin their discourse on Islamic finance with a reference to its special features, as these are what give it a distinctive and superior quality over the traditional modes of financing. A survey of the literature reveals that there are no uniform features in the Islamic approach to finance; an individual's selection is purposive.

Three interpretations of this approach are clearly identifiable, although they do tend to overlap. First, there are those who see the system's humanistic theory and rule compliance as being its distinctive features. Second, there are those who think it is the financial instruments that the system uses that set it apart. Third, there are still others who consider the regulations and procedures that oversee the systems in operation as its distinguishing features. Presently, we shall base our discussion here on the first of these approaches, although we will mention the others in the subsequent chapters.

4 Introduction to Islamic finance

1.3.1 Why not take or give interest?

Islamic finance emerged and derived its strength essentially from the ban the scripture imposed on the institution of interest. After some short-lived controversy over what constitutes *riba* (interest), which Islam declares as unlawful, a consensus has been built around the idea that modern, interest-based financial activities fall within the concept of *riba*. It does not matter whether the purpose of taking or giving a loan is for consumption or production. Nor does it make any difference whether the loan is in the form of money or a commodity. It is this ban on interest that is the most distinctive feature of Islamic finance, and all other features revolve around this ban.

The ban on interest implies that the only legitimate means for survival can be the creation of value in real terms. Islamic finance ensures a close linkage between the real economy and finance, the former dictating and the latter following. The linkage is obvious as, in principle, Islamic financial institutions treat their customers as partners in investment. They cannot sell what they do not own and possess. Economic activities are, by definition, value-creating activities. Because monetary transactions remain asset-based, Islamic finance helps expand the real economy. In essence, the real sector directs the allocation of resources to various uses that financing facilitates. In contrast, conventional finance only requires the existence of real assets as a point of reference. This allows trading in commercial and financial papers as representing pure debt. Thus, mountains of debt grow higher relative to real assets. A legitimate question here is how does Islamic finance account for the time value of money?

1.3.2 Risk-sharing

In recent decades, some writers have assumed the role of a missioner preaching risk-sharing as definitional for Islamic finance; its main departure point from the one based on interest. The oozing is flooding the literature. The idea is like projecting molasses, a by-product coming out of the sugar mills, and labeling it as sugar. The idea is tricky and misleading.

Risk-sharing owes its origin to an old precept in Islamic finance – 'no risk, no gain' – that long stands refuted. In any case, it cannot be defended as an exclusive principle of Islamic finance. Capital owners join a productive effort on a positive note – to earn a profit, risk of loss is its occasional by-product. Thus, risk is not a tradable commodity beyond insurability, nor do we have anything like a risk-sharing contract in financing. The principle of sharing profit and loss is valid, but its basis is not the existence or absence of risk. Factors of production compensated for their ownership of resources. There are many income receipts and gains. And there are activities involving great risks that people undertake that are not for money. The best Islamic response to risk is *tawakal-walil-Allah*. Also, it is wrong to believe that risk in interest-based financing is transferred to counterparties and then financing becomes risk-free. We have seen that during storms like that of 2007, multinational corporations, including banks, collapse like walls of sand.

1.3.3 Time value of money

Money by itself is barren. Marking time alone does not create anything. So, Islam, in general, does not permit putting a time value on money. However, money has purchasing power and has opportunity costs.

This juristic position is the fulcrum of all the deferred obligations on which Islamic finance tends to thrive. For example, this is the basis of the cost plus sale (*murabahah*) with the deferred receipt of price, or leasing (*ijara*). Figure 1.2 shows when money has time value in business transactions and when it does not. By itself, money is barren; it cannot produce even a blade of grass. But it is the most liquid of the assets. It embodies purchasing power and has opportunity costs. It imposes disadvantages on the creditor to the advantage of the debtor. Islam insists on symmetrical treatment for the parties to a transaction. It, therefore, allows time value on money under certain conditions.

1.3.4 Avoidance of gharar

Islam aims at shaping all exchange relations among people on the principle of cooperation, mutual benefit and fair play. It directs them not to expose

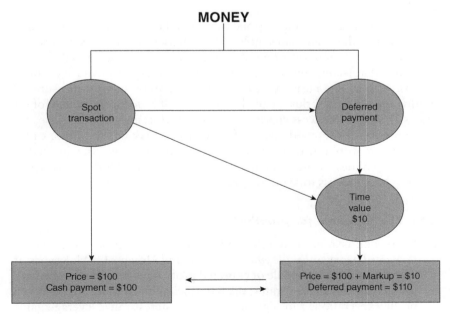

Figure 1.2 Time value of money in Islamic sale.

6 Introduction to Islamic finance

themselves to or inflict on others an injury (loss) that is possible to avoid. These principles lie at the heart of the celebrated Islamic notion of *gharar*, translated as indeterminacy or hazard. Contractual relations must, as far as possible, be free of *gharar*. Prophet Mohammad (peace be upon him) is reported, for instance, to have instructed that fruits on trees should not be sold until they show clear signs of ripening or standing crops should not be sold until the grain ears have turned golden and the danger of damage through natural calamities has reasonably passed. The prohibition on selling what one does not possess at the time of the contract is another example; one may even argue that the ban on speculation also follows from the notion of *gharar*. We now turn, as promised, to an exanimation in some details of an Islamic ban on interest.

1.4 Why ban interest?

The believers required little argument as to why they must shun interest. For them, the instructions of their faith would suffice. In fact, most of the world's religions denounce the institution of interest. It survives because with the passage of time, deviational forces have overpowered the moral sentiment of the followers. However, the resurgence of Islamic finance cannot rely merely on faith for its success because it is in competition with its conventional, interest-based counterpart. Arguments in support of the ban have to be made. Mainstream literature itself provides many of the arguments, but let us begin with a brief explanation of the 'faith position' on interest.

Islam allows the exchange of one thing for the other of its own kind in six cases, including salt, dates, gold, wheat, barley, and currency, only in a 1:1 ratio on the spot or over time. Any excess paid or charged would be riba or interest that Islam bans. If excess is involved in hand-to-hand spot transactions, such as one measure of barley for one-and-a-quarter measures of another type of barley, this is called *riba-al-fadl*. If time for repayment of the debt is allowed, the excess charge is called *riba-al-nasiah*. In either case, it is the similarity of the goods which fall within the six commodities, called *rabawi*. That would attract the prohibition, even if they differ in quality. Different qualities of the same good should pass through the market sale and purchase process to avoid the one-to-one exchange condition.

1.4.1 The rationale for prohibition

1   Writers on Islamic economics find an argument against interest in the *General Theory of Employment, Interest and Money* of J. M. Keynes. It is argued that the schedule of expected profit rates is rarely in tune with the schedule of interest rates, the latter being much more sticky. When profit expectations run high and wide of interest rates, leverage gains

rise because of credit expansion and push up the economy toward inflation. On the other hand, when profit expectations fall faster than the slow-responding interest rates, the economy faces deepening deflation and unemployment. Alternating booms and depressions hinder the long-run growth and stability of the economy. The marginal productivity theory, in addition to its other weaknesses, cannot explain or justify the payment of interest. Islamic economists cannot deny that capital, even if liquid, may inject productive attributes in a factor combination. But more fundamental is the question of whether an interest payment equals or is determined by the productivity of capital. We know that the level of interest rates in a country is essentially determined by the state of its bond market and the manipulation of its monetary policy by the central bank. What has the productivity of capital to do with either of them?

2   All funds – whether owned or borrowed – become inseparably mingled in the business of a firm and are exposed to the same degree of risk in its business. How does the productivity or exposure to the risk of the owned and borrowed components of capital differ from the viewpoint of the firm or society? Why should the two sorts of capital be differently rewarded – one with variable and uncertain profit and the other with prefixed interest? Social conventions or legal fictions need not always be just, and interest is no exception.

3   Interest payments cannot meet the norms of social justice at the macrolevel. Borrowings in the past resulted in the flow of money from the rich to the poor in society. Interest rates were often exorbitantly high, and loans were often required to support the bare necessities of survival. It was the poor who suffered. Today, the situation has reversed in the sense that savings largely come from the middle classes of society, who contribute to pension funds, take out insurance policies, buy units in mutual trusts and put money in fixed deposits. This pool of savings from people with small resources goes to finance the business tycoons via financial institutions. Interest rates are kept low. A policy of cheap money is the order of the day. Small savers part with their money for very little gains (if we consider what they receive as interest) compared to the profits their savings help to generate.

4   Finally, the institution of interest operates against equity financing of business because, among other things, interest payments are treated as cost elements which are allowable deductions for corporate taxes, as opposed to dividends. Thus, the law allows the existence of tax shelters that provide interest that fuels leverage lures with a view to enlarging profits on the asset owners' capital. Tax shelters operate against Islamic institutions, which are in competition with their conventional counterparts. They magnify their taxable profits, other things being equal.

1.5 The rise of Islamic banking

The formal organization of Islamic finance could only begin toward the close of the colonial era, and it gained pace once the Muslim lands had won their independence, mostly after the Second World War. Understandably, its forms, instruments and regulatory framework all evolved and still revolve around the prohibition of interest. The most dominant Islamic financial institutions in the modern era are Islamic banks. We trace their evolution in this book, but, for the most part, the development of Islamic finance, along with *takaful*, Islamic insurance, lags far behind.

Although Islamic banking, along modern lines, emerged around the middle of the twentieth century, it gained momentum after the 1960s with the rise of Islamic revivalist movements across the world. However, the growth pattern and structure of the fast-expanding Islamic finance differs from country to country, and common and cohesive elements are yet to be established. The development of Islamic banking comprises three broad elements:

1 Since conventional banks were the common experience, the pioneers of the Islamic banking system naturally based the theory of Islamic banking on similar principles, with the exception of the ban on interest. Their road map was dominated by much of the colors they saw around them.
2 This led to a mismatch between the compulsions of the structural choice and the objectives that the Islamic ethos expected a financing system to address. Conventional models suited the short-term liquidity needs of trade, industry and commerce, whereas Islamic finance has to prioritize and make resources available for long-term development goals. Structural diversification now seeks to remedy the situation.
3 Islamic banking was conceived as competing with the mature and large Western banks. This led to a convergence of the Islamic system toward mainstream banking practices in terms of product development and regulatory requirements. The pros and cons of convergence for Islamic finance remain a moot point.

The development and growth of Islamic banking and the challenges it faces today, or may face tomorrow, can be better understood and analyzed if these elements are taken into account. Islamic banking, like its mainstream counterpart, is no more than a means of financial intermediation: a 'neutral' means of transmitting funds from those who have them in surplus to those who need them for the parties' mutual benefit. Certainly, Islamic banks also have to play this role, but once we bring their ethical norms and their contribution to Islamic developmental goals into the equation, they have to move beyond mere intermediation.

1.6 Summary

- Finance is the lifeblood of trade, industry and commerce as it imparts liquidity to resources facilitating their more efficient utilization. Finance adds time value to money by allowing compensation for its use. An understanding of the nature, role and significance of money is required to understand finance, conventional and Islamic.
- Money evolved as a social convention to overcome the inconveniences of barter by separating sale of goods from the purchase of goods. The most important thing about money is its general acceptability, which stems from the stability of its purchasing power. It then matters little what serves as money – the glittering gold or clumpy paper.
- Finance – mainstream or Islamic – deals with liquidity – its creation, distribution, management and distribution at the national and international levels via well-oiled systems. It is the lifeblood of trade, industry and commerce.
- Systemic stability is as essential as it is demanding. Financial turmoil is known to have shaken flourishing economies to their foundations overnight.

Note

1 All figures and tables in the book have been prepared by the author.

Chapter 2

Value of money, trade cycles and social consequences

Chapter contents

- Trade cycles: booms and depressions
- Circular flows of money and goods
- Macroeconomic repercussions
- Distributional issues
- Poverty measures and trends
- Public policy and welfare

Learning outcomes:

Studying this chapter will enable you to understand:

- Significance of money in modern economies
- Finance and creation of wealth
- The Islamic perspectives on financing
- The definitional points of Islamic finance
- The operational framework for Islamic finance
- The current status and position of Islamic finance

Preview

Islam banishes interest. This raises two questions contextual to central banking. First, can Islamic banks create credit like conventional banks? We shall argue that Islamic banks cannot avoid credit creation, an imperative for staying in the market where they operate in competition with their conventional rivals. Evidently, the interest rate policy would not be applicable to them as

DOI: 10.4324/9781003366973-2

a control measure. This leads us to the second question: What could possibly replace the interest rate for Islamic banks? In reply, the chapter suggests what it calls a leverage control rate (LCR) as an addition to central banks' credit control arsenal. The proposed rate is derived from the sharing of profit ratio in Islamic banking. It is contended that the new measure has an edge over the old-fashioned interest rate instrument, which it can in fact replace with an advantage. It can possibly be a common measure in a dual system.

2.1 Introduction

We have explained in the preceding chapter how banks can create credit money. However, they can also destroy it the same way; the credit multiplier works both ways. This ability allows banks power to affect the money supply in an economy. This power is limited in the case of an individual bank. For, if it expands credit at a faster rate than others, its cash base would erode until it falls in line with others. But if all are working together in the same direction, the credit manipulation power of the banking system hardly knows limits. The movement of a group of balloons each tied to a light stick with a string observes no bonds, but an individual balloon can move away from the rest only by the length of its string. That length of string for a bank is provided by the cash it carries.

Money measures the value of other goods and services expressed in their prices. But in turn, goods and services measure the value of money: its purchasing power. If a branded shirt sold for Rs. 200 last year is available for Rs. 250 now, its price is up by 25% but the value of the rupee by 20% i.e. $[(1 - 200/250)100]$.

The value of other measures remains unchanged – a day is always of 24 hours, a kilogram of 1,000 grams and a foot of 12 inches, but money is the measure that enters our lives more than any other measure. All the time with fluctuations in prices. If the prices of *all* goods and services over time and space rise or fall proportionately, no one would bother about their fluctuations, albeit the economy would be working at higher or lower price levels. But the real-life situation is different. Prices do not change by the same proportion, nor are consumption packages of people identical. There are virtually innumerable money values.

This calls for measuring the value of money. Price index numbers are constructed to that end. Index numbers are averages linked with percentages with reference to a base like heights in geography. In bare bones, if P_0 is the base year price and P_1 of the current year, their ratio P_1/P_0, measures the change. The average of such ratios multiplied by 100 gives the index number. Choice of a base, selection of commodities and erection of a system of weights are the main steps in the construction of indices. Decisions on these matters are guided by the purpose of constructing an index. But those intended to measure the changes in the value of money are usually the wholesale or purchaser's price index numbers.

However, of late, consumer price indices are increasingly being used for measuring the temporal fluctuations in the purchasing power or value of money.

As price changes affect production, distribution and trade differently, an examination of the price fluctuations on various groups of people and economic sectors becomes vital. These effects are normally studied with reference to booms and depressions, the phases of a cycle linked to recessions and recovery, as Figure 2.1 shows. The change factor is the interaction between the profit and interest rate creeping up, with labor becoming vocal. The slowdown pricks the bubble. The economy gets into recession. Bleak prospects hasten the pace until the economy touches the bottom in depression. It is a strange situation. Machines stand idle while workers sit jobless. Ironically, there is no coal in their house, as there is too much in the market. Public suffering forces the state to take action to put money into the hands of the people to revive demand for goods and services; public projects are launched. Interest rates are cut, subsidies are provided and taxes are cut to allay the fears of a frightened horse – the entrepreneurs. The recovery engine moves slowly but soon gains momentum. Trade cycles wear a multi-facet character, as Figure 2.2 shows.

Inflation, unless it gets out of hand, promotes growth, income and employment. However, it works against social justice, sharpens income inequalities and skews opportunities against the weak. It helps generate mountains of black money and promotes corruption. It makes the rich, richer; the poor poorer. However, it feeds even most of the paupers.

During inflation, all prices do not rise simultaneously, or proportionately. Relative prices change, favoring some, punishing others. The producers in general gain. Output prices rise faster than the expense items – profit margins increase. Manufacturers gain more through capacity increase, efficient organization and political clout than the agriculturists – land cannot be

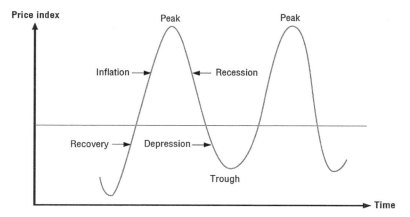

Figure 2.1 Phases of a trade cycle.

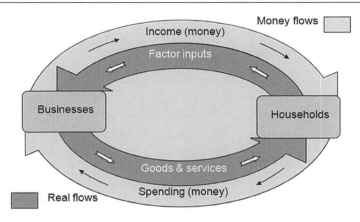

Figure 2.2 Real and money flows in a two-sector, closed economy.

stretched; intensive cultivation is restrictive. Organized workers gain; unorganized ones lag far behind. Those in the entertainment industry gain the most. The fixed-income groups like renters, teachers pensioners, interest earners and domestic help tend to suffer.

Depression is indeed depressing – there is gloom all around. The situation is rather paradoxical. Machines stand still; workers sit idle. The efficiency of the system remains the same as before the crash. Entrepreneurs need to produce; people need goods. Why then does the system not respond? Is it not working? Psychology: it is easy to slow down a galloping horse pulling the reins but difficult to assuage the fears of a frightened horse to move forward despite flogging. It takes time. Thus, the peaks of the cycles are longer and the turns sharper; in contrast, the bottoms are broader and agonizing. Intervention was needed. A crop of central banks grew across countries after the 1930s Great Depression with powers to manage the money supply in the country; monetary policies were designed to control banks' credit creation lure.

If the creation of credit tends to fuel leverage lure, causing injurious fluctuations in the economy, why not ask banks to keep with them at all times the legal tender (base) money people deposit with them? This is the same as the insistence of some Islamic economists for a 100% reserve system, instead of the fractional. Of late, one hears some supporting voices for the proposal albeit faint in the mainstream economics as well. This looks neither operable nor expedient. The demand for a 100% reserve must create rigidity in money supply response to the genuine seasonal ups and downs in money demand; it may even result in as much trouble if not more as the current fractional reserve system unleashes.

One compelling reason for allowing banks to operate on fractional reserves is that it facilitates the adjusting of the money supply to the seasonal variations in money demand. Figure 2.3 shows how credit creation

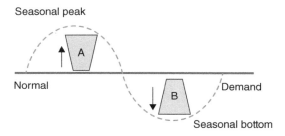

Figure 2.3 Seasonal variations.

keeps demand for money commensurate with the normal base money supply in the economy (Hasan 2014, 42–43). Thus, credit creation is an economic imperative and Islamic banks need not be denied the option to promote their survival. Anyway, they have had to fall in line with the global practices here as also elsewhere. Monetary authorities in various Muslim countries and the International Finance Service Board (IFSB) are seized with the issue: the regulatory frameworks are being revamped and new standards are being designed. Credit control has to be part of the exercise. As Islamic banks replace interest with profit rate, let us see how such a rate comes into existence.

Islamic banks replace interest with profit rate; let us see how such a rate comes into existence

2.2 Key measures

The measures central banks use for credit control are well-known. Broadly, they attack the base of credit creation – cash the banks carry. One of these is that banks must keep a minimum ratio of their deposits as reserve with the central bank, the Reserve Ratio (RR) we have already mentioned. An increase in this ratio reduces the creation of credit deposits and vice versa. The second is the 'open market operations'. Here, to expand the credit base, the central bank buys first-class securities the banks hold in the market to put more cash in their coffers; it sells them to do the opposite.

The success of the measure depends on the response of the commercial banks: they may not, for example, consider it more rewarding to move into securities and out of cash. The central bank also has limitations. It must sell securities cheaper when their prices are rising and buy them high in a falling market. It loses in either case. How much loss can the central bank absorb?

Interest is embedded in the open market operations. How would Islamic banks operating in a dual financial system respond, even as securities could be sorted out as compliant and noncompliant? The question goes a begging in the Islamic finance literature. Presumably, they would fall in line, as most of them are already benchmarking their profit margins on interest rates. We have suggested recently a new weapon of credit control as an addition to the arsenal of the central banks – the LCR. The reaction of the scholars and the practitioners is awaited. Let us reiterate our suggestion here briefly.

2.3 A new measure mooted

This measure is based on the presumption that the major incentive for credit creation banks catch upon originates outside the system – in the lure of leverage gains borrowers enjoy. It further assumes that there would always be a rate of profit in the economy for the borrowers corresponding to the prevailing rate of interest. In a two-tier mixed *Mudarabah*, profit sharing applies to earnings that are allocable to the part of capital K a bank provided to the firm. Thus, if P were distributable profits, λP would be allocable to the bank, the pure financier. It is this part of profit that is the subject matter for sharing with the firm. The parties would negotiate to reach the fraction of that profit say y^* that will go to the bank and the remaining $(1-y^*)$ the firm will retain for the entrepreneurial services it rendered to make bank money earn a return. Applying the same mechanism of bargaining between the bank and depositors will give the bank a part of the depositor's profit (Tier 1 in Illustration 2, Appendix).

The fraction of profit λP going to the bank y^* could be equal to, more than or less than its loss-sharing ratio λ. But the fraction of total profit P would always be less than each of y^* and λ. As, $\Upsilon P = y^* \lambda.P$, $\Upsilon = y \lambda$. Since both y^* and λ are less than 1, their product must be less than either of them. This derivation of ϒ allows the treatment of the ratio issue at the macrolevel and helps the construction of models to show, as in Equation (2.1), that the profit-sharing ratio (PSR) is a function of four variables – i.e., the expected rate of profit π on capital K, the proportion of borrowings λ in K, the market rate of interest r_i and the risk premium or economic profit α.

$$\gamma = \frac{\lambda}{\pi}(r_i + \alpha) < 1 \tag{2.1}$$

Figure 2.4 shows that in duel financial system market forces will eventually lead to a compatibility between the PSR and the market rate of interest.

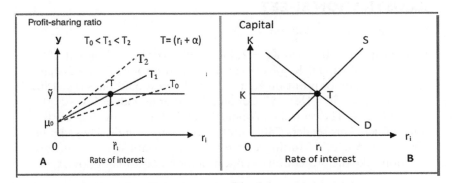

Figure 2.4 Profit-sharing ratio in a state of equilibrium in an Islamic economy.

Equation (2.1) provides us with a commonsense and useful link between the PSR of the banks and the rate of interest in a dual monetary system. It follows from the equation that in a competitive setting, the sharing ratio γ for the bank at the macrolevel varies inversely with profit expectations π and positively with the other determinants λ, r_i, and α. Now, we change the explanation of these variables with reference to the Mudarabah contract between the banks and their depositors so as to forge a credit control measure for Islamic banks. From Equation (2.1) we get

$$\frac{\lambda}{\gamma}\left(r_i + \alpha\right) = \pi < 1 \tag{2.2}$$

We know that business firms can garner more profits for their owners – the equity holders – when profit rates run higher than interest rates; loaning from banks becomes attractive for leverage gains that raise returns on equity. However, bank loans are of short duration, not exceeding three months. They are suitable for financing inventories or at best plus a part of working capital. But the gains are increasingly alluring, leading unabated to the conversion of short-term financing to long-term project financing through a roll forward via renewals. Such rolling is welcome to banks as well. But it is perilous and has led to financial crises, big or small.

Islamic banks, like the mainstream ones, are not barred from creating credit in the mainstream, nor are businesses free of leverage lures. Here, we suggest an instrument for the central banks to dampen this lure. This we designate as the leverage curbing ratio or the LCR symbolized with B. How would the measure operate in a dual financial system? Its linkages to other variables in Equation (2.2) have been explained and illustrated comprehensively in an earlier paper (Hasan 2016). Here, we need not repeat the process. Suffice it to say, LCR would have a restrictive effect on businesses' lure for leverage gains. This would tend to force up their PSR with the firms, which would further dampen the lure. Banks, too, would fall in line.

ILLUSTRATION SHEET

(Amount in million dollars)

Equity capital of the firm KF = 2,000; Bank loan BK = 1,000 at 18% interest; Total capital K = 3,000 Profit earned on K = 750; KF share 2/3 = 500; Rate of profit on K, π = 25%; Interest paid on KD = 180; Profit on KF = 750 – 180 = 570, or 38.5%. Leverage gain = 570 – 500 = 270 or 13.5%. The central bank puts the LCR, B = 5%, making π + B = 30% on KF. This renders 750 – 600 = 150 as free funds. They can be diverted to Auqaf, a Muslim country that may establish social welfare functions like the promotion of education or eradication of poverty

The LCR can operate in harmony with the usual measures central banks use for credit control. Variations in the ratio can help banks wisely distribute financial resources. In this regard, the ratio can have a helpful interface with fiscal policies – taxation, subsidies and exemptions.

2.4 The risk-sharing ruckus

Sharing of investment risks by the capital owner is projected continually since the turn of the century in the literature as the definitional postulate of Islamic finance. The frequency of assertion is on the increase after the demonstration, rather inconclusive, that Islamic banks faced the 2007 financial turmoil better than the mainstream banks that promote risk transfer, not sharing. The postulate did not go unchallenged. However, instead of answering the queries raised, the proponents choose to blow their trumpets louder, more frequently.

The postulate is highly restrictive. If capital faces the risk of shrinkage, workers risk their limbs and lives while working on machines, apart from health hazards they face manning, for instance, the burning furnaces or oil rigs in the open seas. Soil erosion can render land less fertile at no fault of the owner, and the managers may have reduced leisure. The point is that all factors of production are exposed to some sort of risk, and their risks are neither measurable nor comparable.

Furthermore, does Islam *always* disallow pre-fixed return on investment under all circumstances? Are the profit-sharing schemes entirely free of risk transfer? Are they invariably equitable? Or, is the interest-based financing entirely risk-free? Questions of the sort remain unanswered, but must be answered.

To begin with, the postulate is based on a rather restrictive interpretation of a leading Islamic maxim derived from a Prophetic tradition; it says, "Benefit goes with liability". The problem here is with the proponents' interpretation of the word 'liability' in the statement as the bearing of risk in financial transactions. Islam does count profit and loss-sharing contracts among the valid modes of financing. But risk bearing is a consequence – not the cause – of such contracts. To put it straight, there is no such thing in Islam as a risk-sharing contract that, when entered into, would result in the sharing of profit or loss. Liability in the maxim focuses on compensation, not on risk; for risk is not a tradable commodity.

Risk-taking per se cannot contribute to production. This is why gambling is banned in Islam. Ownership of useful things, including capital contribution to production, deserves a reward. Equity of a profit share can be better judged with reference to capital investment, not with reference to risk. The contention finds support from another Islamic maxim, an inverse of that under discussion.

It says, "Liability accompanies gain". The maxim is derived from the Qur'an:

> Those who swallow usury will not rise, except as someone driven mad by Satan's touch. That is because they say: commerce is like usury. But God has permitted commerce, and has forbidden usury. Whoever, on receiving advice from his Lord, refrains may keep his past earnings, and his case rests with God. But whoever resume are the dwellers of the Fire wherein they will abide forever.
>
> (2:275)

There has to be compensation for receiving a gain. Thus, for a claim to profit, a financier is liable to bear ex post loss not the ex ante risk (Al-Sadr 1984).

Conventional finance is of course dominated by interest-based transactions, but it is far from the truth that it never entails risk-sharing. Equity holders share risk and equity dominates in long-term financing. Even when loans are advanced on interest, banks face the risk of default and of adverse price movements in collaterals. That banks collapsed like a house of cards in the 2007 turmoil is evidence enough to see that interest-based finance is not always or entirely risk-free. Likewise, Islamic banks do transfer risk via hedging contracts. They also take collateral to cover default risks.

The bulk of transactions Shari'ah supervisors approve are debt based; participatory finance, despite all efforts and pleadings, is still not popular. The valid distinction between Islamic and conventional finance is not that one is entirely risk-sharing and the other is entirely risk-transferring; the deciding factor is their proportion in the mix. Furthermore, it is not true that Islam bans risk transfer. It is a matter of interpretation. Banning interest does not imply an automatic ban on risk transfer. Indeed, there is an argument that in pure classical *Mudarabah* where the worker/entrepreneur is empty-handed, the financier transfers a part of his risk to the worker. The financier does not make any payment to him in case of loss. He reduces his own loss equal to the transfer earnings of the worker; in a way, risk is in part passed on to him (El-Gamal 2014, 1).

Likewise, risk-sharing need not always be equitable; presumably, it is rarely so. Risk being ex ante has no cardinal measure. The sharing ratio is a crude proxy for the division of profit. No one can demonstrate a one-on-one correspondence between the profit share of the parties and their risk exposures. Justice and fair play are the first requirements for calling something 'Islamic'. The difficulty is that tons of juristic writings analyzing contract forms provide little help to determine whether or not there is injustice in the exchange contract. Arbitrariness rules.

Furthermore, Islam grants payment for owning factors of production – land, labor and capital – contributing to the output of permissible goods.

It does not tie payments to risk that all factors face in the course of production in some form and measure. Moreover, it allows many fixed payments like salaries, rental, fees, commissions that entail no risk. On the other hand, it disallows others infected with much risk, like those laced with *gharar*, chance games, smuggling, theft and trading in non-halal goods.

Finally, it is incorrect that the mainstream banks remain immune to risk, or always transfer them to other parties. The history of financial crises testifies that the giant mainstream banks and insurance companies crumbled like sand walls in storms that occasionally swept across the globe.

2.5 Concluding observations

We set out to examine the work and efficacy of the measures the central banks seek to control the credit creation activities of the commercial banks in a country to deal with the resultant leverage gains luring modern businesses. In the process, we have mooted a new weapon for their arsenal – the LCR. It is a cost-free measure and deals with the issue simultaneously at both ends – the demand and supply sides of loanable funds. The LCR works in harmony with the usual credit control measures; it supplements them, clashing with none.

Islam allows earnings that may not entail any risk, and it disallows others who do. Risk is a by-product of productive contracts; it is not tradable in itself. Islam advises guarding against risk, but eventually, patience and *tawakal* are the Islamic response to all adversities. I admire Tawakal as the name of a hospital in Malaysia.

Risk bearing got attached to capital as an exclusive attribute during the centuries of the mercantilism march with profit being its reward for cooperating in producing wealth. Adam Smith saw the Industrial Revolution led by capital accumulation knocking at the British door. In his *Wealth of Nations*, he gathered the bricks to raise capitalism as an economic system nurtured by the great proponents that followed. The seamy sides of capitalism, especially the exploitation of the working classes and the spread of pauperism, were soon unveiled and socialism led by Marx as an alternative with operational demonstrations also emerged. However, the time lag, ideological divisions, and operational handicaps left it in the lurch. Economies across the world have fast been sucked in by the increasing versions of the capitalist system.

Muslims have been attempting to erect a version in an Islamic framework. There has been little success on the theoretical front, none on the ground, save a shade in the area of Islamic finance. Here, too, some with international connections continue flogging the old horse: "No risk, no gain", to keep the cosmopolitan linkage intact. We have already demonstrated the naivety of their stand in this chapter.

2.6 Summary

- Money measures the value of all real goods and services, called their prices. We can measure the general level of prices through the construction of their index numbers.
- Value of money varies inversely to variations in the index. But all prices do not vary in the same direction or proportionately. Price level variations change relative price structures.
- The changes in the price level or the value of money affect different population groups differently. The tendency of the general price level to continue rising is called inflation, or falling deflation.
- The alternate occurrence of inflation and deflation is designated as business cycles. There are numerous theories explaining why they take place.
- Both inflation and deflation are equally undesirable if either gets out of hand. Within limits, inflation is better, though it aggravates distributional inequalities; deflation is worse because it contracts output, income and employment.
- The central bank controls credit that banks create to feed business lure for leverage gains. Islam approves the measures the bank uses for the purpose of replacing the profit rate for the rate of interest. An additional tool is also added.

Chapter 3

Islamic finance
The basics

Chapter contents

- Islamic finance and its growth
- Systems convergence
- Internationalization of Islamic Finance
- Comparative performance
- Islamic banks and financial turmoil
- The gold dinar echo

Preview

Islamic economics as a formal academic discipline has been on the scene for over four decades, but its development has been patchy, deficient and oblique. It could not make much progress on the theoretical front or policy implementation except in the field of finance – Islamic banking has risen as a bright star on an otherwise dark firmament. It has grown beyond the boundaries of the Muslim world to impart duality to the financial systems in over 90 countries across the globe. Islamic banking has matured fast. It has been challenging mainstream banking as a viable and better alternative in its own citadels for its welcome characteristics.

However, fast growth has brought problems too for Islamic banking. It is quickly converging with its mainstream counterpart. In this process, it is seen as being subsumed by the bigger system. Product designs are imitative; innovations are rare. Interest and its compounding in the return on capital seep in for the ease of the noncompliant, uniform installment payments. This chapter discusses such issues and those they bring forth in Islamic finance.

DOI: 10.4324/9781003366973-3

3.1 Introduction

Islamic finance has a bright future. Muslims are at present the second largest religious community in the world – every fourth person in the world is a Muslim. Their rate of growth is also the fastest, mainly because of conversions – reports are that Muslims will be the largest of the religious communities by the middle of the century. A more contributory factor is that religious commitment and cohesion are on the rise among the faithful. Figure 3.1 is revealing.

Notice the fertility rates in Muslim countries have been on the lower side – between less than two to three – and tend to fall in many cases. The yellow international cutoff at three is the outer limit; still, many countries, including India, have reported higher fertility rates. In the first two decades after the turn of the century, the Muslim population has grown at twice the global increase.

Islam is the most rational of all religions – conversion, not fertility, is swelling numbers, as Table 3.1 shows. Thus, the market for Islamic finance is assured and expanding.

It is not just the fast-expanding market for Islamic finance in Muslim countries; its systemic merits are attracting adherents across the world. Islamic financing emerged 50 years ago, in countries with large Muslim populations who were keen to see that their source of funds was governed by the requirements of Shari'ah and the principles of Islamic finance. However, Islamic finance was spreading fast across countries. Its rate of growth doubled in 2019 despite the pandemic. Islamic finance assets amounted to US $2.88 trillion, recording the highest growth for the industry since the 2007 global turmoil. There were three contributory factors: (a) the appreciation for the role Islamic finance plays in *responsible* investing; (b) its geographical choice of markets where interest in Islamic finance is gaining prominence; (c) digital transformation, which makes Islamic investments more accessible (Figure 3.2).

3.2 The basics

Financial markets are often seen as a means of equilibrating savings and investments and allocating investment over time and space, with banks **acting as intermediaries** between savings and investments. Financial markets are in principle deemed to be detached from the real economy.

In contrast, the definitional feature of Islamic finance is its intimate linkage with the *real* economy – that is, with the production of the usable goods and services the religion allows, not the often advocated risk-sharing. All the other traits of Islamic finance follow this basic tenet and so do its departures from the mainstream financial system. Let us illustrate.

For the year 2019, the reported estimates in trillion US dollars were: stocks 70.75, bonds 199.8, derivatives 640 and the nominal gross domestic

Islamic finance 23

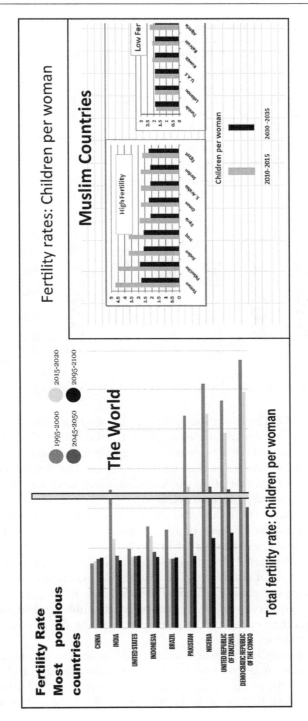

Figure 3.1 Fertility rates.

Table 3.1 Muslim versus world population growth

Entity	Population (billion)*		Rate of growth
	2000	2020	
World (a)	6.114	7.795	27.5
Muslims (b)	1.291	2.000	54.9
(b/a) 100	21.12%	25.66%	200%

* Source: World Development Reports

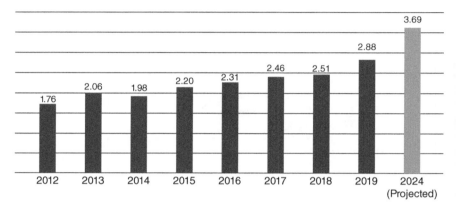

Figure 3.2 Growth of Islamic financial assets (trillion US dollars).

product (GDP) 87. The first three put together, worth about $911 trillion, constitute the global size of purely monetary transactions and pitch against the size of the value of real goods and services, the GDP for the year. Thus the monetary sector was more than ten times bigger than the real economy. Islamic finance would not allow such a wide divergence and its perilous consequences, especially business cycles.

Business cycles, as we understand them today, were unknown until the first French economist Clément Juglar identified them in 1860. They must have been nonexistent in the era when the barter system – commodity for commodity – dominated economic activity. No mismatch between the demand and supply of goods could be sustainable. Business cycles surfaced after money tore the coin of exchange into selling and buying separately, working as the go-between. The separation created independent, unmatching layers in modern economies of money and goods, the monetary dominance ever increasing.

The real economy is concerned with the flows of production, purchase and consumption of goods and services like autos, bread, and haircuts within an economy. In contrast, financial economy refers to transactions that involve purely money or monetary assets in trading. The sale and purchase of stocks, bonds, debt, futures or their derivatives are some examples. Monetary transactions of the sort far outstrip the real economy transactions – 70 times some estimate.

If we work down the chain of any such transaction, we may eventually find some real good at the bottom. However, Islam is averse to such distant associations. Even though some heterodox jurists are trying to provide justification for such transactions. Islam demands close, visible contact. The demand dictates its character.

3.3 Main features

Financing activities that comply with Shari'ah – the Islamic Law – are referred to as Islamic finance. It includes the provision of short-term liquidity and the long duration of permissible investments. The main features and procedures of Islamic finance did not evolve over time and space like the conventional. It starts on a positive note. It accepts what the mainstream contains minus what Islam does not permit plus what the divine requirements are exogenous to the system and start from negativity. Thus, the Islamic financing arrangements are to comply with the following instructions.

3.3.1 The ban on interest

Shorn of the finer point of the debate on what interest is, all religions of the world, including Hinduism, disallow it. However, there is a lack of consensus among the jurists and practitioners on what it is that Islam prohibits. The disagreement on bank interest is widespread. Some leading jurists in India and outside permit it. The central bank of Iran regulates interest rates both for short-term finance and long-term investments. It controls insurance companies as well.

Most Islamic economists agree that the prohibition applies to all loans – individual or institutional, in the form of money or commodity, and taken for consumption or production. Notable is that not only is the charging of interest banned but its acceptance as well. Thus, many believers either keep their money in interest-free deposits or donate interest income to social welfare projects.

3.3.2 Factors and profit sharing

As all capital – owned or borrowed – is exposed to the same sort of risks and uncertainties within the business of a firm, Islam allows them to join hands on the basis of equality – the sharing of the results. It ordains joint venture (*musharakah*). Banks in Turkey have, indeed, made much headway in promoting participatory finance.

26 Islamic finance

To us, participatory finance has been of wider ramifications. Output is the result and measure of the *combinational* productivity of – capita and labor – the factors of production. The marginal productivity theory of J. B. Clark attempted to separate them illogically – by assuming one factor constant and varying the other to attribute the increase in output to the latter. In most cases, factors are complementary; they cannot be varied in isolation of each other. For driving nails into wood planks in furniture making, you cannot increase a hammer without adding a worker to use it. It may not be possible even in the case of the same genus. You may hold the lower blade of a scissor and move the upper to cut paper. But it would be false to claim that the cutting is being done by the upper blade as the lower one is all the time there to support it. They are not distinct in their presence but only in their activity – one is dynamic, the other still at the time. Thus, marginal productivity is arbitrary, the combinational real. Economic profit – a surplus over cost – must, therefore, be shared between capital and labor. Here is a macro-model.

Let Y be the aggregate value product of the business firms, P the profit, W the minimum wage and T the business taxes. Thus,

$$Y = P + W + T. \tag{3.1}$$

Suppose P is shared between capital and labor in the k and (1–k) ratios, respectively, where k is an institutional variable. We have

$$Y = kP + (1 - k)P + W + T. \tag{3.2}$$

However, the market wage, say W, already paid to the workers will invariably be more than the minimum wage W. Equity demands that the excess amount paid to them must be adjusted to their share of the profit (1 – k) P. Equation (3.2) then becomes

$$Y = kP + \left| (1 - k)P - (W - W) \right| + W \pm T. \tag{3.3}$$

Let us put | (1 –k) P – (W – W) | = B, where B may be called the bonus payable to the workers. This gives us the final distribution equation conforming to the Islamic spirit and intent:

$$Y = kP + W + B + T, \tag{3.4}$$

where kP is to be shared by the capitalists among themselves, (W + B) goes to the workers, and T to the state. In the case of individual firms suffering losses, B may well be negative. This may be debited to a special account to be charged

Islamic finance   27

(i)   against the workers' future share of profit, or
(ii) to the reserves built through deductions from P prior to its distribution.

In the model, P is the net of business taxes, and a mutually agreed policy of profit retention may be enforced to take care of the financial requirements of the industry. The more inquisitive may perhaps like to ask, But what is the theory involved in the scheme of the model? It is the sharing principle. The problem is how the k would be fixed. Well, let a consultative be formed, perhaps for each industry.

3.3.3 The ban on interest

Taking of interest is considered a sin not only in Islam but in all religions. That Islam bans not only taking but acceptance of interest as well is clear. However, what it is that Islam bans is not so clear. The interest banks charge on loans has especially been in dispute. Some leading jurists in India and abroad have allowed it. Most Islamic banks across countries work on a profit-sharing basis. Participatory banks as they are called in Turkey have flourished in that country.

Iran is an exception. Banks charge interest. The central bank of the country regulates interest rates on short-term advances, as well as on long-run investments. Insurance also falls under its control.

Islamic financial theorists and practitioners agree that the ban applies to all sorts of loans in the form of money or commodity, meant for production or consumption. The return of the principal, even of the dead, is sanctified. The prophet (peace be upon him) is reported to have declined to lead the funeral prayers of one until some companion cleared the debt of the deceased.

Notable is that not only is the charging of interest banned but also its acceptance. During my 25 years of service in Malaysia, the universities were assigned to open account banks that did not pay interest on deposits. In places where interest on deposits is paid, the faithful must donate the receipts for permissible social welfare activities.

3.3.4 Non-investible businesses

Islam identifies businesses where the faithful cannot invest their money; these are the goods Muslims are barred from producing, selling and consuming. A broad categorization is as follows.

3.3.4.1 Involving speculation (maisir)

Shari'ah strictly prohibits any form of speculation or gambling, which is called *maisir*. Thus, Islamic financial institutions cannot be involved in contracts where the ownership of goods depends on an uncertain outcome.

28 Islamic finance

Chance betting was disallowed. Horse races were an exception, presumably to encourage the raising of better breeds for warfare. Oman still remains the largest supplier of quality horses the world over.

Presumably, taking a cue from this exception, some Islamic jurists are searching for a justification to condone trading in futures and derivatives to see Islamic finance no less fruitful than the mainstream. The endeavor looks perilous.

3.3.4.2 Those infested with gharar (indeterminacy)

Islamic finance bans participation in contracts with avoidable uncertainty to future outcomes to the disadvantage of either of the parties. The edict followed the prophetic tradition that directed the believers not to sell fruits on trees unless they show signs of ripening or standing crops until the ears have turned golden and the danger of damage by weather change has reasonably passed off.

The principle of gharar is of wide application and may cover a variety of foul play and cheating in business. A cement plaque on the highway between Alexandria and Cairo reads, "Don't wet cotton before selling". It is a crime in this world and punishable in the hereafter.

To safeguard against gharar, there is the instruction to the seller to give the customer a little more than the measure. I saw this tenet of Islam operating in the market culture in Iraq during my employment there from 1981 to 1982. After full measure, the shopkeepers invariably added a little more. I must state an interesting incident related to this norm.

Among us working in Iraq, we had one Prof. Mehta from Gujarat. One day, he narrated his predicament to us thus: I get meat daily from a shop but the seller refuses to accept payment. Surprised, we two accompanied Mehta the next day to the shop. He asked for his usual measure. The shopkeeper packed and waived his hand to us go. We asked for the payment.

"Free for miskeen (poor)".

"He is not miskeen; he is a professor".

"Professor", he exclaimed in awe. "Why he buys so little, just 250 gram?"

"He lives alone, family is not with him".

"Still", he murmured but accepted the payment.

3.3.4.3 Inviting unethical activities

Islamic banking shuns investments in alcohol, gambling, pork and other forbidden items. However, it is not that mainstream financing is unconcerned with ethical norms in the investing of funds. It is on record for preaching the refrain against investing in industries like the chemicals that may harm the neighborhood.

Indeed, there is a sizable overlap in the Islamic and non-Islamic ethical spread where the two financing systems can supplement each other.

Examples are reduction of inequalities – social and economic, eradication of poverty, meeting basic needs of the deprived or improvement in greening, and so on. Islamic finance has visibly delivered in these areas in some Muslim countries. For instance, Pakistan leads the world in environmental care. Malaysia is known for meeting basic needs and reduction of inequalities in incomes.

Socially Responsible Investing (SRI) avoids putting money in controversial areas, such as gambling, firearms, tobacco, alcohol and drugs. Some examples of ethical funds are as follows:

- Environmental, Social and Governance Funds
- Impact Funds
- Faith-Based Funds

The availability of reliable information to act is a must for the success of the SRIs. Institutions providing information for decision-making owe a responsibility to the general public regarding their reliability. For example, accountants provide information about companies that allow the public to make investment decisions for retirement, a child's education and major purchases such as a home. For people to rely on the information provided, there must be a level of confidence in the knowledge and behavior of accountants. Ethical behavior is necessary in the accounting profession to prevent fraudulent activities and to gain public trust. Such ethical commitments are all the more crucial in the case of public sector undertakings and in the assessment of the government's fiscal performance. Indeed, this extends to the entire gamut of social management in a democracy. This creates many dilemmas for honest operators and professionals like editors, anchors, accountants, jurists and politicians. At times, their lives are at stake for speaking the truth in corrupt political systems dominant across the world.

3.4 Growth for development

Islam is not an ascetic religion. Planet Earth, with all its treasures, Allah has put under human management. Adam is the divine vicegerent on Earth. Mankind – not Muslims alone – is the inheritor (2:29). And Allah raises or depresses whom HE wants without distinction. Muslims were promised to be the dominant community provided they followed the "Straight Path". Thus, the Glorious Qur'an exhorted them to pray: O' our Lord, give us what is the best in this world and give us what is the best in the hereafter. The scripture links the two; it spells out how mundane achievements can be made the means for spiritual solace. Imbibe that charity increases wealth while interest reduces it.

Islamic finance promotes growth with stability through maintaining a firm link with the real sectors of an economy and adherence to ethical norms. There is no divorce between what finance demands and what the real economy aspires for. They move in close circuitry as Figure 3.3 depicts.

The inseparable link between financing and the real economy in the Islamic system economizes on fund use. One must expect the release of funds stuck in purely monetary transactions for boosting the production of welfare-promoting goods and services, easing in the process, the credit management tensions of central banking. The Islamic financial systems, like others, can influence the allocation of resources and hence economic growth. Highly liquid markets for stocks, bonds and demand deposits transform financial instruments helpful for long-term projects. An additional advantage of the linkage is the improvement in the ability of the system to withstand financial crises. There is empirical evidence to testify that Islamic banks showed better resistance to the 2007 turmoil.

Global Islamic assets expanded by 10.6% in 2020 against a growth of 17.3% the previous year. Currently, the industry is worth USD 2.25 trillion (4 May 2021). Thousands of publicly traded Shari'ah-compliant companies operate today in tens of countries worldwide.

A recent research talks of the impact of the global financial systems in the Arab world on Islamic finance; on its principles and practices in particular. It recommends uniformity in global Islamic standards and an improvement in accounting practices.

Since the late 1980s, discussions on economic development have seldom avoided adding 'sustainable' to the argument, even though there is scant agreement on what sustainability is or what it is that must be sustained.

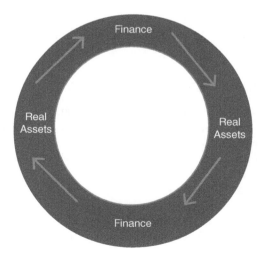

Figure 3.3 Islamic finance: The nominal-real circuitry.

However, one thing is very clear in this haze: Each vision of sustainability converges on environmental concerns.

The continuous urge for an increase in the output of goods and services to raise the living imposes a trade-off between material prosperity on the one hand and pollution poisoning humans on the other. Regrettably, the latter is winning. Here is an area, and a noble cause, for the mainstream and the Islamic financial systems to work together. Environmental is a *maqasid* concern.

3.5 System convergence

The abolition of interest and the promotion of growth with equity were the conceived goals of the Islamic system. These goals expressed a long-run vision to improve the condition of the Muslim communities across the world. However, the organizational forms adopted for Islamic finance were mostly of the existing mainstream commercial banks which provided short-term loans on interest to trade industry and commerce. The choice thus involved an intrinsic mismatch between the structure and objectives of Islamic finance. The mismatch did carry some advantages, but on a more important side, it exposed Islamic finance to commitments and influences which could not go with the goals the pioneers of the system had in mind.

The mismatch forced a unidirectional convergence on the Islamic system in competition with the mature conventional finance the West dominates. It is not the ground realities that are being made to wear the Shari'ah norms; it is the norms that are being stretched to the limit for meeting the demands of the conventional system. The mainstream is subsuming the Islamic system. Imitation, not innovation, dominate product designing/formulas are used for the ease of uniformity in the installment payments to clear loans with little knowledge that such installments of necessity involve the compounding of return on capital, apart from importing some other un-Islamic consequences. The lament is that Shari'ah scholars of repute approve of their use, ignorant of the implications. Muslim masses full of reverence for Islamic finance stand cheated, bankers and the jurists benefit.

Thus, what Islamic finance can or cannot achieve depends on where its ongoing unidirectional convergence to the conventional system leads it. Currently, most merits, claimed for the Islamic system, defy evidence.

3.6 Islamic finance and the turmoil

The 2007 financial crisis downed many mighty banks, even governments, in the West over the next five years or so. this period has emerged the contention that Islamic banks have faced the crisis better than the conventional, testifying to the inherent strength and resilience of the system. This strength follows from a close link between financial flows and productivity

32 Islamic finance

in the real sector of the economy. Not a few Islamic economists then claimed that this property of Islamic finance contributed toward insulating it from the potential risks resulting from the excess leverage and speculative financial activities that are the root causes of the current financial turmoil. The factors mentioned may have possibly kept Islamic banks less affected, but one cannot ignore certain other factors which may have softened the impact of the crisis on Islamic banks. Consider for example the following points.

1 Islamic banks are still too small to attract the contagion because of their tiny existence; the ratio of Islamic banks' assets to conventional banks was just 1:164 in 2011, even as it has been improving over the years. It has overall been climbing up.
2 Islamic banks have not yet developed enough connectivity with the mainstream system for the transmission of contagion. Even then, it is not true that all Islamic banks remained unaffected by the crisis. It is on record that several banks plus Nakheel in the United Arab Emirates did come to grief and the government had to bail them out. Kuwait refused to help its failing banks.
3 Most comparisons employ econometric models where sample designs and the reliability of data are dubious, as their homogeneity over time and space carries serious question marks. In particular, contagion within the banking system is a smaller matter than the overall effect of the turmoil on the totality of the economic phenomena. The injury to banks is not the result of financial market chaos; it is just its reflection. It is the consequence of wide and wild lurching of the broad macroeconomic variables – national income, savings, investment, money supply taxation, wage levels and so on. Figure 3.4 is revealing on the point.

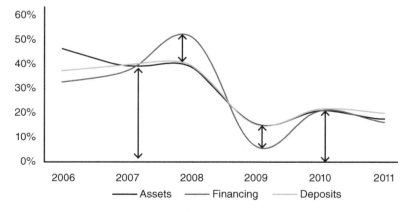

Figure 3.4 The 2007 turmoil and Islamic finance.

3.7 The gold dinar echo

Among the contributory factors to the American invasion that downed Saddam in Iraq and Gaddafi in Libya, some count the declared intention of both leaders to quote the oil price in gold not in dollars, as was the practice. For the move had the potential of bringing the fall from the pedestal of the mighty dollar worldwide, along with serious erosion of its gold piles.

In Malaysia, the astute politician Mahathir Mohammad presumably wanted to gauge the potential of this policy weapon. No state action in this regard could be advisable. An academic feeler was launched in the guise of reviving the gold dinar as a Muslim world currency. In no time, there was an inundation of literature – books, articles, monographs – a tribe of scholars was around, speeches, seminars and discussions were rampant – reason and emotion distinction lost distinction. Even a mint was erected in an eastern state of Malaysia, triggering the coinage of the gold dinar and the silver dirham. Mine was alone the dissenting voice in the big noise.

An international seminar was held on gold dinar in 2004 at the IsDB headquarters in Jeddah. Bank Negara, Malaysia and experts from a dozen Muslim countries were invited to participate. I traveled to that seminar on my own because of my conviction that the introduction of the gold dinar was neither desirable nor feasible at the moment. M. U. Chapra was present for Saudi Arabia. I had prepared a ten-page note for the seminar spelling out my opposition to the proposal. This note became the basis of discussion as no other write-up was available. Not much discussion took place. My argument prevailed. The proposal was shelved as inopportune. The main points of the note were as follows.

- The religion never divided money into Islamic and non-Islamic. The Prophet did not debar the circulation of the pagan-era coins that carried the images of their idols.
- Muslim countries were not having sufficient gild to support conversion to meet the balance of payments deficit that the Muslim world as a whole was then chronically having with the rest of the world.
- The ills the fiat money is charged with are misplaced. It is not money but its mismanagement and political corruption where the blame lies.
- Last, but not least, the International Monetary Fund (IMF) had amended its rules as early as 1979 to add a clause that no member country could link its currency to gold. Evidently, if Muslim countries had to deal with the IMF or the World Bank, they could not defy the rule to have the gold dinar. The proposal died, presumably forever.

3.8 Summary

- Islamic finance has a secure and expanding market due to the fast-growing Muslim population and increasing popularity across the world.

- The basic characteristic of Islamic finance and its point of departure from the mainstream is its linkage with the real economy, not the sharing of risk. From this tenet, follow its other features.
- The main features include a ban on interest, avoidance of gharar, investment in permitted industries and activities only, profit share for labor and the promotion of development.
- The 2007 financial turmoil affected Islamic banks as well, albeit to a lesser extent.
- The concept of the gold dinar has long become obsolete.

Chapter 4

Contracts and instruments

Chapter contents

- Contracts and institutions
- Maxims relevant to finance
- Participatory modes and instruments
- Determinants of sharing ratios
- Islamic banks and equilibrium ratios
- Demand and supply of funds impact
- Time and modes division

Preview

In Chapter 3, we discussed the main principles of Islamic finance and its dos and don'ts. It is logical that we now take a look at how these principles shape contractual relations and the modus operandi of Islamic finance. We begin with an explanation of the juridical maxims that govern Islamic finance and draw its contours. As profit sharing is basic to Islamic finance, we explain its participatory structuring and modes and their temporal division.

Sharing raises many ticklish issues, important being the determination of the sharing ratios in two-tier participatory finance operating in completion with the powerful international interest-based financial system that it aspires to replace. The determinants of these ratios have been identified; how they attain equilibrium status and respond to the demand and supply pulls for funds is explained.

4.1 Introduction

Interest, because of its prefixed character, is a unifying influence on thought, principles and practice in conventional finance. This character *per se* is not

DOI: 10.4324/9781003366973-4

36 Contracts and instruments

the reason for its abolition in Islam, as wages of labor and rent of land, too, are prefixed elements of cost in business. Interest is singled out for abolition because it generates various sorts of injustices in society and perpetuates them. However, its abolition has for the present left Islamic finance looking conceptually weak. The literature on the subject shows, for instance, much avoidable confusion in the usage of the terms 'principles', 'contracts' and 'instruments', whose divergent and overlapping explanations abound. 'Principles' guide the shaping of the contract. 'Contracts' are agreements between parties based on their free consent, reciprocal consideration and status as a lawful object. 'Instruments' are the documental outcome of contracts that are salable in the market. Perhaps the term *'mode'* better unifies the implications of the three terms. Naturally, Islamic arrangements had to be interest-free. Initially, this anxiety moved thinking away from the fixed return modes of financing. Islamic banks, unlike conventional banks, could not depend on lending activities or the extension of credit on interest. Earlier writers thus had an exclusive commitment to equity-based financing modes – *mudarabah* or *musharkah*. The modes giving fixed returns to investors had to wait for approval until almost the turn of the twentieth century. Today, the modes that Islamic institutions use for financing are classified into two broad categories:

1 Participatory modes where finance is provided *directly* to the projects. The modes include *mudarabah/musharakah* and *muzaarah*.
2 Modes that provide finance *indirectly*, such as by trading are based on a generic notion of sale and involve the deferment of one liability under the contract – either the payment of the price or the delivery of goods – to a future date. *Murabahah* and its variants fall in this category.

The modes of Islamic finance are derived from Islamic jurisprudence. The corpus of juristic or legal *maxims* provides the guidelines that help to structure these modes and also facilitate their validation under varying conditions. The discussion that follows on maxims liberally draws on the work of Professor Hashim Kamali, a well-known jurist in the area of Islamic finance. A maxim is a *general* rule that covers all thematic ramifications. It is taken as a self-evident truth that requires no proofs. Legal maxims are theoretical abstractions in the form of short expressions conveying the *maqasid* (goals) of *Shari'ah*. They improve our understanding of the *Shari'ah*. Maxims were evolved gradually in parallel to the development of *fiqh* (Islamic jurisprudence). They vary with the level of abstraction and scope. Some apply to *specifics*; others are of a general sort. Five of those falling in the generic category are called *normative* maxims and apply to the entire gamut of *fiqhi* issues without distinction; they capture the essence of *Shari'ah* as a whole. The remaining ones have stemmed from these five maxims. For example, a person is considered innocent of a charge unless and until the charge is proven; the benefit of the doubt always goes to the accused.

Contracts and instruments   37

The implication is that a certainty can be overruled only by counter-certainty. The maxim is usually applied in criminal cases, but it can be invoked in civil suits as well. In one case, Abbas promised a mosque that he would donate a specified amount of money by year-end. The trustees, relying on the promise, undertook a contract with a builder for repairs. Abbas later backed out of his commitment. The trustees lost the case in the lower court on two grounds. First, the trustees could not prove to the satisfaction of the court that the promise was ever made. Second, there was no consideration (compensation) involved, even if the promise had been made. On appeal, the High Court reversed the judgment. The evidence the trustees produced regarding the promise having been made was held to be acceptable and the argument of consideration was overruled as the trustees had their intention to use the money for repairs known to Abbas. Thus, Abbas had to pay the money plus a fine. (Abbas and mosque in this illustration are fictitious).

4.1.1 Legal maxims

The five legal maxims of significance in the present context are as follows:

a   *Matters will be judged by their objectives (Al-Umur-bi-masidha)*: The principle rests on a *hadith* which says 'Actions are but by intentions'. This maxim can be better explained by allowing what is not permissible normally. Suppose a ship is carrying both goods-in-trade and passengers. It is caught in a storm and it is necessary to reduce the weight of the ship to keep it afloat. It would be lawful under these circumstances to throw part or the whole of the cargo overboard because it is far more important to save the lives of the passengers.

b   *Haram shall be removed (Al-Dararyuzalu)*: Islamic law completely shuns that which causes *haram*. If it is not possible to avoid *haram*, a smaller *haram* is preferred over a larger *haram*. The maxim follows from the *hadith*: 'There must be neither *haram* nor the imposition of *haram*' [Sunan al-Daraqutnî (3:77), al-Mustadrak (2/57) and Sunan al-Bayhaqî (6/69)]. The principle protects the buyer from *haram* in the sense that the goods purchased under a sales contract must be free of all defects, latent or patent. For instance, when A buys a house and discovers later in the rainy season that it has a leaking roof, A has the option to revoke the purchase contract.

c   *Certainty shall not be removed by doubt (Al-Yaqin la yazulu bi-al shakk)*: This follows from a major axiom of Islamic law that things are legally assumed to remain as they are unless and until it is established with certainty that they are otherwise (different). Extraneous doubts are of no consequence [Sharh Sahîh Muslim (4/49)].

d   *Hardship shall bring alleviation (Al-mashaqqahtajibu al-tasir)*: This means that the existence of hardship demands its removal to effect ease. Indeed, this maxim is the epitome of the Qur'anic declaration in verses

38 Contracts and instruments

such as "*God intends for you ease and He does not intend to put you in hardship*" (2:185), and "*God does not intend to inflict hardship on you*" (5:6). This is why in Islamic finance, banks are instructed to be considerate to the defaulters in meeting their contractual obligations and extend time for the discharge of the debt preferably without penal action.

e   *Custom is the basis of judgment (Al-aada al-muhakkamah)*: The maxim comes from the saying of a companion – what Muslims (collectively) deem to be good is good in the eyes of God. Thus, *mudarabah*, *musharakah*, metallic coins and slave labor, etc., continued according to custom for centuries in Muslim countries. Likewise, when a contract is silent on a matter, the court can base its judgment on *current* and *predominant* custom provided that the matter is not regulated by the text and the custom does not conflict with the provisions of the *Shari'ah*. For example, when a garden is leased to a person so that he/she can benefit from its produce over a period, the law assumes that the person will take care of the garden and maintain it as is customary in the region, even if the norms are not stated in the contract. It comes about that what is customary and familiar is presumed to apply even though it is not in the contract.

4.2 Participatory modes

Early writings on Islamic economics were influenced by its historical legacy, which had viewed direct or participatory finance as being based on profit-and-loss-sharing (PLS) as the sole mode of operation. Essentially, these included *mudarabah* and *musharakah* for business and *muzaarah* as their counterpart in agriculture. The implications of the sharing system at the theoretical and applied levels are in a state of continual exploration. The distinction between *mudarabah* and *musharakah* is not very clear in juridical pronouncements, but it is possible to identify two differences.

First, *mudarabah* is more suitable for projects of a relatively short duration and a specific purpose, such as the construction of roads, bridges, shopping centers and so on. *Musharakah*, on the other hand, is the general sort of equity participation in ongoing businesses.

Second, in *mudarabah*, the profit-sharing ratios (PSRs) have no relationship to the loss-sharing ratios of the parties. In *musharakah*, the two can be identical. For this reason, the participation of the financier in the decision-making process of business may differ. It is interesting to note that divergent PSRs are not confined to *mudarabah* alone. In conventional partnerships the PSRs are in general proportionate to the capital contributions of the partners, but this need not always be the case; the agreement may, and at times does, specify a different ratio for any of the partners. Thus, there are resemblances between *mudarabah* on the one hand and modern partnerships on the other. It is, therefore, understandable why jurists often

Contracts and instruments 39

use the two terms – *mudarabah* and *musharakah* – interchangeably to explain the *modus operandi* of the PLS system. In our discussion, we use a model based essentially on the *mudarabah* PLS features. In *mudarabah*, financiers assign their resources to some productive activity through an entrepreneur in exchange for a share in the returns on *that* investment; financial losses – if they arise – fall entirely on contributors of the capital. The external financiers will have no role in the management of the business. The jurists generally agree that in *mudarabah*, resources can be contributed in the form of money or money's worth. As the PSR is negotiable between the entrepreneur (firm) and the financier (bank), a ticklish issue in Islamic finance is how this ratio is determined. We now consider its solution.

4.2.1 Ratio determination

We begin with how the PSRs would be determined between the business firm, the entrepreneur, and the bank, the financier. To keep matters simple, we assume as follows:

1 The firms and the Islamic banks operate in a competitive dual financial system where the conventional banks provide, in competition, funds for business on interest.
2 The firm and the bank both aim to maximize their profits.
3 There are no taxes or transaction costs.
4 The profit expectations of a firm and the loaning bank concerning a given investment coincide.
5 There are no market impediments to adjustment to changes in the variables.

We fix the following symbols to facilitate the analysis:

K Total capital employed in the project
λ Proportion of K provided by the bank
P Profit earned including interest
α Risk premium as fraction of K
r Rate of profit earned on K ($P = rk$; i.e., $r = P/K$)
ri Rate of interest

In *mixed mudarabah*, the bank provides part of the capital invested in a business expressed as λK. In addition, λ also gives the ratio $(1-\lambda)$ as the leverage measure for the firm and helps to specify its owners' portion in total profit P. Of course, any losses will be shared between the firm and the bank in the same ratios as their capital contributions, i.e., $(1-\lambda)$ and λ, respectively.

Profit-sharing applies to earnings that are allocable to λK, the part of capital K that a bank provides to the firm. Thus, if P were distributable profits, λP would be allocable to the bank finance. It is this part of the profit that will be shared with the firm. Negotiations between them lead to the decision that a fraction σ* of this amount will go to the bank and the remaining part (1 − σ*) will be retained by the firm for the entrepreneurial services it rendered to make the bank's money earned a return. It is easy to see that what goes to the bank is a smaller fraction of the *total* profit P than σ* because σ* λP, the bank's profit share, divided by P would equal σ*λ. In σ = σ* λ, with both σ* and λ being less than 1, their product σ must be smaller than either of them. Here we derive a variable σ that would allow the treatment of the ratio issue at the macrolevel. The model will show that the PSR is a function of the variables symbolized earlier as the expected rate of profit r on capital K, the proportion of borrowings λ in it, and the market rate of interest ri and the risk premium fraction α. Figure 4.1 provides an illustration.

Let us assume that the firm in the illustration is typical of the industry and has the option of seeking finance from any source, Islamic or conventional. What is the minimal profit expectation, under our assumptions, that could possibly bring the firm to an Islamic bank? Arguably, the firm must expect to receive such a proportion of profit as would promise the same or a higher return on its investment as it would obtain in going to an interest-charging financier. But it would be willing to accept even less in order to compensate the bank for sharing the financial risk. Thus, for the firm, we may show this as

(1 − σ) P ≥ P − riλK − αλK (dividing both sides by K, and solving we get the share of more than what the firm shall not be willing to offer the bank).

$$\sigma \leq \lambda / r [r_i + \alpha] \tag{4.1}$$

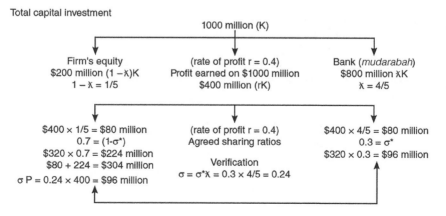

Figure 4.1 Process of profit sharing under the mixed-mudarabah system.

Now let us look at the issue from the viewpoint of the bank. It will not participate in financing the project if its PSR is not expected to yield a return that will at least equal what financing with interest is giving to conventional banks, plus a premium for the risk of loss involved in the participatory finance. Thus, we have the share for the bank as follows:

$\sigma P \geq r i \lambda K + \alpha \lambda K.$

Dividing through by K and solving we obtain the share more than or at least equal to what the bank won't agree to accept.

$$\sigma \geq \lambda/r\left[r_i + \alpha\right] \qquad (4.2)$$

A look at Equations (4.1) and (4.2) suggests that

$$\sigma = \lambda/r\left[r_i + \alpha\right] \qquad (4.3)$$

would alone satisfy both parties. Figure 4.2 helps explain the determinants of the ratio σ.

If we put $\lambda/r\,[r_i + \alpha] = \beta$, the PSR
β for appropriate adjustments in its constituent elements, except r varies inversely.

Points 'a' and 'b' in Figure 4.2 not being on the curve β_1 depict states of inequality between the demand and supply of investment funds. At point 'a' the sharing rate for the bankers is higher than their expectations; they

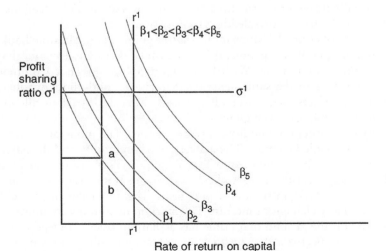

Figure 4.2 PSR determination for the bank.

42 Contracts and instruments

would tend to increase loaning. Competition among the financiers will force a reduction in σ forcing it back to equality at β_1. The opposite would happen at point 'b' when the demand for funds would exceed their supply.

4.3 The instruments

The instruments of Islamic finance must comply with Shari'ah requirements in form and substance. Also, they must be rooted in real goods and services. Their temporal division into short or long run is contextual to purpose. The same instrument can be used for either duration, albeit relative suitability may differ. For example, murabahah is more suitable for financing consumer durables and musharakah for business. Sukuks are preferable for long-term debt financing. There may be special-purpose designs.

4.3.1 Murabahah

Murabahah is a financing structure where the seller and buyer agree to the cost and markup of an asset, the markup replacing interest that Islam bans. This renders murabahah an acceptable form of credit sale in Islam. This cost-plus instrument has numerous varieties used widely in Islamic banking. However, the position of commodity murabahah is murky.

Commodity murabahah is one of the most commonly used financing contracts in Islamic banking. It belongs to the deferred contracts group. Here, the bank buys a consumer durable like a car or home and sells it to the client on periodic installment payments on an amortization plus basis. We shall discuss such threadbare contracts in the following chapter. The successful completion of such contracts poses no problem. With these contracts usually being long term, breaches sometimes do take place, giving rise to disputes of various sorts, leading to litigation.

A number of court decisions in the matter going against Islamic banks in Malaysia have confused people. It is being asked if commodity murabahah defies Islamic requirements. We believe, in principle, it does not. Commodity murabahah falls in the same generic category of 'uqud almu'awadhat' or exchange contracts that cover all types of transactions Islam allows. In exchange contracts, a given quantity of one commodity is traded for a given quantity of another commodity, including money. The monetary value of a commodity is called its price. The delivery of a commodity and the payment of price may not be simultaneous. The obligation of one of the parties may be deferred to a future date. A client may, for example, request a bank to purchase a car for him on a cost-plus basis. The arrangement per se does not contain any element of interest. The markup in commodity murabahah is allowed on the ground that "time has a share in price". Indeed, it is this juristic pronouncement that justifies the deferring of obligations in Islamic contracts. Even the courts did not throw out the cases in Malaysia on a juridical basis; the structuring of contracts was to blame.

4.3.2 Musharakah

It is a joint enterprise or partnership structure in Islamic finance in which partners share in the profits and losses of an enterprise. *Musharakah* is a form of shirkah al-amwal (or partnership), which in Arabic means "sharing." Although all partners have an equal right to participate in management, any partner may waive the right of participation in management and leave it for any other partner willingly. The partners can provide their part of the capital in money or in money's worth. Their profit and loss-sharing ratios may differ.

Musharakah mutanaqisah is an important variant of the contract. The partnership is between two parties in which one partner gradually buys the whole or parts of the property, usually via installment payments. Banks use it to finance home purchases in preference to other modes. We revert to examining the form and working of this variant in the following chapter.

Istisna is generally a long-term sales contract between a customer and an Islamic bank whereby the bank agrees to construct and deliver an asset at a predetermined future time, at an agreed price. The customer makes the payment to the bank either in installments or at delivery or after the completion of the project.

Ijara is a lease contract. It is an Islamic technique for financing the construction or manufacture of assets on Shari'ah-compliant terms. Here, the lender agrees to buy the asset to be delivered once construction or manufacturing of that asset is complete, on a rental until the cost is paid in ways as per agreement.

Wakala is an agency contract whereby the wakil acts as the agent to carry out a specific job on behalf of the financier, the principal for an agreed payment.

Sukuk is the Islamic equivalent of a bond, although rather than a debt claim, the investor owns a share in the underlying asset. The Sukuk structure has been used on a number of project finance transactions in the Middle East.

Waqf, donating land or other assets for public social welfare projects like wells, inns, graveyards, highways, or educational institutions has played a significant role in the economic development of Muslim lands. Indeed, it is rightly regarded as the third (voluntary) sector of the economy. A recent addition to the instrument is the cash waqf.

4.4 Sharing and investment

Sharing magnifies the fear of shrinkage of capital and detracts from the incentive to invest, slowing growth and development. This charge on Islamic finance often comes from Western writers: sharing makes Muslims risk averse. How valid is this charge? Apparently, the charge looks arbitrary, if not partisan. The proponents have never produced an objective,

44 Contracts and instruments

convincing evidence. What makes sense is that more capital could make one more venturesome – less capital, less. In addition, it is more a matter of one's attitude toward the peril, not its sharing. Risks of war are more frightening than of business, and the evidence of the past and present has shown the believers braver. Islamic law and tradition take the gains and losses of business as the will of God.

It is reported that one Friday Caliph Umar (may Allah be pleased with him) was addressing the believers after the prayers. A man came running and whispered to him, "The ship that was bringing your good has sunk".

"Alhamdolillah", said Umar and continued his sermon.

Soon came another person informing him that the earlier news was wrong, and the ship has safely docked at the port.

"Alhamdolillah", said Umar and continued.

After he had finished, a man sitting near the dais who had heard the reports, asked, "Ya Amirul-momeneen; how it is that you thanked Allah whether the news was good or bad?"

The will of Allah is always a divine blessing for the believers and one must always be grateful to Allah: this is tawakal.

4.5 Summary points

- Participatory modes of finance – *mudarabah/musharakah* and *muzaarah* – provide financing for the projects directly. On the other hand, the modes that provide finance *indirectly*, such as by trading, are based on a generic notion of sale and involve the deferment of one liability under the contract.
- Certain juridical maxims are to be observed to validate all sorts of Islamic financial modes, procedures, and instruments.
- Islamic finance is based on the sharing of profit agreements; loss is always shared by the capital owners proportionate to their contributions. The sharing of profit ratio is influenced by several factors, including, among others, the rate of interest and ex ante profit.
- The profit-sharing principle needs to be extended to sharing with labor as well.
- The contention that Islamic banks are risk averse is hypothetical, if not partisan.

Glossary

- ➤ **Marginal productivity** of production factors is illusory and indeterminate. Its isolation is arbitrary.
- ➤ **Islamic maxims** are the consensual juridical edits governing the behavior of the believers in all walks of life.
- ➤ **Risk aversion** is an opinioned and unquantifiable concept. Tawakal is the Islamic response to gain or loss.

Select references

Hasan, Zubair. (1983). Theory of profit: The Islamic viewpoint. *Journal of Research in Islamic Economics*, King Abdulaziz University, Islamic Economics Institute, Vol. 1, No. 1, pp. 3–14.

Hasan, Zubair (2002). Mudarabah as a model of financing in Islamic banking: Theory, practice and problems. *Middle East Business and Economic Review*, Vol. 14, No. 2, pp.41–53.

Tatiana, N. (2015). Principles and instruments of Islamic financial institutions. Science Direct. https://www.sciencedirect.com›science›article. Accessed on 20 August 2021.

Chapter 5

Financing consumer durables

Chapter contents

- Hone financing: need and nature
- Musharka-Mutanaqisa Program (MMP)
- Installment determination formula
- Juridical weaknesses of MMP
- Zubair Diminishing Balance Model (ZDBM)
- MMP–ZDBM comparison

Preview

Owning a home is a lifelong ambition for many. Homeownership instills in one a sense of achievement, peace, and security. But most people did not have enough money in a lump sum for fulfillment until the early decades of the preceding century. Mortgages as a source of home financing appeared on the scene no earlier than 1930. Interestingly the idea originated not with banking but in insurance.

A *mortgage* is a loan wherein the house one buys functions as collateral. The financier, now mostly a bank, is the mortgage lender that loans the client a large chunk of money – typically 80% of the home price – which must be paid back with interest as per an agreed time span. Failure to pay back the loan allows the lender to take the home back through a legal process known as *foreclosure*. The client can occupy the house for use. Thus, he contracts an in-home mortgage.

Islamic banks use the same tools as the mainstream to arrive at the periodic installments – amortization of capital plus a return on it – markup or rent. Mortgage-based loan contracts between the parties – the bank and the customer – have to be certified by a competent panel of jurists as Shari'ah compliant. The typical position the jurists take is that they are not

DOI: 10.4324/9781003366973-5

concerned if the process of installment determination is working or if its subsequent impact meets the Islamic requirement or not. They examine and certify only the compliance of law by the content of the contract presented to them for certification. To the jurists, this looks skeptical. Contextually, we reexamine in this chapter the nature of the installment determination of the leading model of home financing, comparing the Musharka-Mutanaqisa Program (MMP) with the proposed alternative, the Zubair Diminishing Balance Model (ZDBM)

5.1 Introduction

People with limited means in developing economies can seldom afford the outright purchase of consumer durables like homes cars or computers. One way to acquire such expensive consumer goods is the hire purchase arrangement where the buyer makes an initial down payment and pays the balance plus interest in easy installments. However, under hire purchase, both ownership and purchase are delayed until payment is completed. Another option banks offer is sale on installments, where the sale is complete and the ownership passes to the buyer subject to the provisions of the agreement. It is observed that pricing in the latter case tends to be higher. Islamic banks mostly go by installment financing.

In cases where contracts culminate successfully, the choice of the arrangement turns out to be a matter of taste, not of substance. However, the asset purchase contracts are of longer durations. Contracts may run over the decades in the case of home purchases. Breaches can and do take place. Examination of a contract cannot ignore the consequences of a breach for the parties from a juridical angle. In our view, two investigations are needed.

- Have the uniform installment payments been free of the compounding of return on capital that Islam pointedly denounces?
- Has the ownership of asset ratio all along been commensurate with the payment ratio?

I first raised these queries and presented my views on the subject to the academic community at INCEIF where I was then working; I also put it on their blog, *Thought Leadership*. The presentation had to face some sharp criticism from peers and some leading Islamic bankers of the country who were among my PhD students. I stood my ground and continued putting my views across in my writing; the first authentic article appeared in the reputed *ISRA Journal of Islamic Finance* (2010).

I tried to engage some of the current juristic lights in the discussion, but instead of shedding the light, they chose to put off the lights. An interesting incident is when a young Saudi jurist saw me sitting in the first row of the audience and whispered to the compeer to announce that the question-answer session was open to students only, not to teachers. But the jurists

48 Financing consumer durables

have to provide satisfactory answers as to why they have been certifying as advisors the contracts containing un-Islamic elements to legitimize the fees they charge for the work.

I am not a jurist by training or profession. I may commit interpretive errors. I am open to correction. Until this happens, Islam gives me the right to ask questions. Nay, orders stopping the wrong. After all, what modes Islamic banks are using to finance consumer durables like homes may not all be valid; they are not God ordained. So, let us examine them once again. As the MMP has replaced most other home financing methods in Islamic banking. We will examine this program and ZDBM, which we propose to replace it, with reference to the queries we have raised and beyond.

5.2 The MMP

The model uses equal periodic installments like the commonly used equal monthly installments: the equal monthly installments (EMIs). These installments combine part payment for the return of capital and part for the return like interest on it. However, the formula Islamic banks use to determine the installments, being the same as the mainstream banks, use *equal* installments that compound the return to capital, be it interest, markup, or rent. *We cannot get rid of this un-Islamic blemish unless equal installments are made unequal.* The ZDBM alternative structure is free of this fault.

I have been highlighting the violative character of the MMP and the edge of the ZDBM over it in my writings for over a decade. There has been little opposition to the ZDBM; their focus remains on defending the MMP for the uniformity of installments; they insisted that the model is Shari'ah compliant. Islamic jurists argue that how banks got the installment amount is immaterial if the mortgage contract is otherwise law-abiding. Most of the argumentation is now part of the literature on Islamic finance. Still, our challenge to the proponents of the MMP stand. Be they academics, bankers, or jurists.

The proponents fail to see the seamy side of the MMP that comes out loud and clear once there is a breach of the contract for any reason. Home financing being long run, contract breaches are expected and do take place – cases in thousands are pending in courts in Malaysia. Let us reexamine the MMP structure vis-à-vis the ZDBM performance.

Given the amount of loan given (P_O), the chargeable rate of return (r), and the time units involved (n), Islamic banks mostly use the following formulas to determine the installment payment (A) and the end period receivable amount (P_n):

$$A = P_0 \frac{r(1+r)^n}{(1+r)^n - 1} \tag{5.1}$$

$$P_n = P_0 (1+r)^n \tag{5.2}$$

Once the installment amount is determined using this formula, it is immaterial from the juristic viewpoint how the proceeds are subsequently divided between capital amortization and profit earned on it. In the expression $(1 + r)^n$, 1 denotes capital, r the chargeable rate of interest, and n the number of time units involved. Thus, the expression tells us how much capital (= 1) would become in n time units. To illustrate, let the rate of interest 'r' be 10% or 0.1 per unit. In the first year (n = 1) capital – i.e., 1 would become (1 + 0.1) = 1.1). The bank treats 1.1 as capital for the next period (n = 2) and multiplies it by (1 + 0.1) to get 1.21. Now, if the loan amount were 100, it would become 100 * 1.1 = 110 in the first year and 110 * 1.1 = 121 in the second. If the rate of interest were a simple noncompounding charge, 100 in two years would grow to 100 + 10 + 10 = 120. Thus, compounding in the first case adds 1 to the total because it converts the first-year interest = 10 into capital for the second-year interest on it being 10 * 0.1 = 1.

It comes about that compounding capitalizes interest (income). Islam regards interest as a curse; compounding is even worse. It converts the poor into paupers. Nay, it has even humbled the rich, downed the mighty banks, and bankrupted nations. Seemingly low rates make loans snowball. Apparently, manageable debts grow into mountains of misery. In many cases, countries find their GDP insufficient to service the debt, let alone pay back the principal! England has to pay no less than $42 billion a year just to service its debt (BBC News, Business, May 2012). Pakistan's debt predicament is the latest example.

Regrettably, Islamic banks use the same formula in home financing for determining periodic installments as conventional banks do. Their leading design is the MMP. In this model, the client and bank enter into an agreement to jointly buy the house of the former's choice. The client contributes part of the sale price, and the bank pays the balance. Both become owners of the house in the ratio of their contributions. The house is assumed as if on rent at the market rate. The client buys back in installments the share that the bank owns. To show that this model and the conventional design are identical in form and results, we construct a case assuming the facts as follows (see also Table 5.1).

Cost of the house $100,000
Customer pays = $20,000 as his part of the initial cost
The bank pays the balance – i.e., $80,000 ($P_0$)
Interest/rental rate = 8%
Semiannual 4% or 0.04 a unit
A = $5,886.54
The following values have been derived using the formula in Equation (5.1).
Semiannual payment: A = $5,886.54
Semiannual rent: R = $ 4,000
Number of installments: n = 20
Total payment (P_n) = A * n; P_n = $117,730.80

50 Financing consumer durables

Table 5.1 Worksheet the parties have based on the illustration data

Installment	Return of capital	Balance outstanding	Return on balance C 4%	Installments	Compound element
A	B	C	D	E = B + D	D* 0.04
0	0	80,000	3,200.01	5,886.54	128.00
1	2,686.54	74,519	3,092.54	5,886.54	123.70
2	2,794,01	71,674	2,980.78	5,886.54	119.23
3	2,905.76	68,592	2,864.55	5,886.54	114.58
4	3,021.99	65,449	2,743.67	5,886.54	109.75
5	3,142.87	62,180	2,617.95	5,886.54	104.72
16	4,838.81	21,367	1,048.23	5,886.54	41.19
17	5,032.84	16,336	854.71	5,886.54	34.19
18	5,233.11	11,103	653.43	5,886.54	28.14
19	54442.44	5,660	444.11	5,886.54	17.76
20	5,660.13	0	226.41	5,886.54	9.06
Total	80,000	94,4270	37,730.85	117,730.80	1,509.80

5.2.1 Compounding

Compound element enters installments because the formula capitalizes the preceding period's return on capital – interest or rent – adding it to the following diminishing balance. The diminishing balance is arrived at as follows:

$B_n = B_{n-1} (1 + r)^n - A$ (n here is installment number)

Figure 5.1 explains the process using the data from our exercise.

5.2.2 Waiver of compounding

Recently RBI, the central bank of India, directed commercial banks to grant waivers of compounding the interest from the EMIs the borrowers pay to redeem their loans to enhance their relief in view of Coved-19 hardships. However, such awaiver is not possible unless the uniformity of the EMIs is sacrificed – equal installments are made unequal.

Compounding occurs through the capitalization of the periodic interest payments. To determine the current period outstanding loan balance (P_n), the interest charged on the preceding period balance (P_{n-1}) is added to it before deducting the EMI. Thus, we have the current period balance:

$$P_n = P_{n-1} + P_{n-1} (1 + r)^n - EMI.$$

Compounding is evident from the second term of the equation.

Consider the following illustrative exercise. Suppose that $50,000 is borrowed at a 12% annual rate of interest payable in 5 years – i.e., in

Financing consumer durables 51

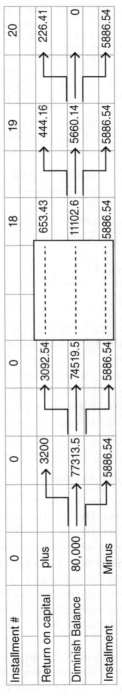

Figure 5.1 Compounding enters all home financing where the EMIs are uniform.

52 Financing consumer durables

Table 5.2 Waiver of compounding must make EMIs unequal

	EMI	Balance	R on C	R of C	Com	Waiver
n	A	B	C	D	E	F = A − E
1	1,109	50,000.00	500.00	609.00	5.00	1,104.00
2	1,109	49,391.00	493.91	615.09	4.94	1,104.06
3	1,109	48,331.39	487.76	621.24	4.88	1,104.12
58	1,109	2,431.00	35.17	1,073.93	0.35	1,108.65
59	1,109	13,46.31	13.46	1,084.57	0.34	1,108.66
60	1,109	261.17	13.59	1,095.41	0.14	1,108.86
Total	66,540	16,805.80	16,803	49,737	168	66,372

60 months. The monthly per unit interest rate being equal to 12/1,200 = 0.01, the monthly installments will be calculated as follows:

$$EMI = 50000\frac{0.01(1+0.01)^{60}}{(1+0.01)^{60}-1} = 1109.$$

This information helps generate Table 5.2. Column E indicates the compounding element in the EMIs. Its waiver must make EMIs unequal, as column F shows.

If the EMIs are to be kept equal, the only way of benefiting the borrowers to the extent of compounding the interest they pay is to make periodic refunds outside the system. For example, a loan contract may contain a stipulation that the lender would return the compounding amount – as in Table 5.2 – at the end of each year.

5.2.3 The Bay Bitehamam Ajil variants

Currently the BBA – sale with price deferment – has found much favor with the banks for safety reasons. The contract in practice has two variants. In Malaysia, it has an embedded buyback (*inah*) provision. The customer books the house with a developer with some earnest money, committing to pay the balance within an agreed period, and ownership is transferred to him. During this period, he sells the house to a financing bank at cost price with a simultaneous contract to buy it back from the bank at the cost plus a markup he agrees to. The house is pledged with the bank as collateral. The amount becomes a debt payable to the bank as per an agreed installment payments scheme.

In Bahrain, murabahah replaces inah. In either case, the banks face little risk in this structure. In case of default, they are amply covered by the pledge, and the down payment may be forfeited. In contrast, the customers are all the way on the receiving end. In the case of installment delays, there is a penalty clause that can be invoked, even though under regulations, the amount must go to a charity fund the bank has to establish for that purpose. The main source of trouble is the treatment of the whole buyback amount as debt. Banks insist that whatever the time point of default, the debt remaining unpaid has to be cleared in full. More disquieting than default is the situation when debt is all cleared before maturity but the banks still do not waive the profit component for the remaining period.

5.3 The ZDBM

Leaving aside the finer legal, structural, and regulatory positions of this general frame, we can spell out the working aspects of the ZDBM. It is based on three mutually exclusive and independent contracts to be consecutively executed on the juridical constructive liability principle (Table 5.3).

- A sale contract among the customer, bank, and the seller giving co-work as the agent of the *bank under an appropriate letter of authority*.
- A contract whereby the bank sells his share to the customer with an agreed 8% markup over cost – $80,000.
- A contract whereby the customer mortgages the house with the bank until the installments have all been paid in full.

The first of these contracts is based on the principle of ***constructive ownership***; ***constructive*** ownership refers to implied or virtual ownership of something tangible for the benefit of another person. For example, in many countries, a broker may have effective ownership of company shares owned by an ordinary investor because the broker alone can buy and sell shares on the stock market that the investor directly cannot. Likewise, civil laws allow spouses to be in constructive ownership of each other's property or of their children.

Figure 5.2 is a schematic depiction of the ZDBM's contractual setting.

Table 5.3 Working of the diminishing balance model

Installment # n A	Return of capital B	Outstanding balance C	Return on capital 4% D	Installment payment E = B + D
0		80,000	–	–
I	$4000	$76,000	$3200	$7,200
2	$4000	$72,000	$3040	$7,040
3	$4000	$66,800	$2880	$6,880
...	...	...	...	...
I9	$4000	$4,000	$320	$4,320
20	$4000	$0	$160	$4,160
Total	**$80000**	**$84,00000**	**$33600**	**$11,3600**

54 Financing consumer durables

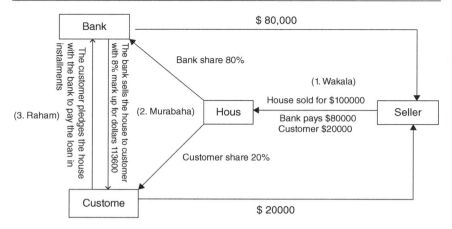

Figure 5.2 ZDBM structure – contracts, parties, and their interconnections.

Table 5.4 ZDBM and MMP: Comparative position (amount $)

n	Outstanding balance		Return of capital (R of C)		Return on capital (R on C)	
	ZDBM	MMP	ZDBM	MMP	ZDBM	MMP
	A	B	C	D	E	F
1	80,000	80,000	4,000	2,687	3,200	3,200
2	76,000	77,313	4,000	2,794	3,040	3,093
3	72,000	74,519	4,000	2,908	2,880	2,981
4	68,000	71,612	4,000	3,023	2,720	2,864
5	64,000	68,590	4,000	3,144	2,560	2,743
16	20,000	26,197	4,000	4,840	800	1,047
17	16,000	21,357	4,000	5,034	640	853
18	12,000	16,325	4,000	5,235	480	652
19	8,000	11,091	4,000	5,445	320	442
20	4,000	5,647	4,000	5,663	160	224

Table 5.4 depicts the comparative position of the two models.

It is the contract of mortgage between the customer and the bank that survives to the end – i.e., till the effects are fully cleared in any mode of home financing conventional or Islamic. Mortgage under the ZDBM, apart from being compounding free, has some more advantages over the MMP mortgage.

5.4 Ownership transfer comparison

An un-Islamic consequence of the MMP in addition to compounding is that the rate of ownership transfer to the customer remains less than the rate of

Financing consumer durables 55

Table 5.5 Ownership transfer versus payment rate

Semiannual units	1	2	3	4	5	6	7	8	9	10
Payment rate %	5	10	15	20	25	30	35	40	45	50
Ownership rate %	3.35	6.85	10.48	14.36	18.19	22.27	26.52	30.94	35.54	40.32

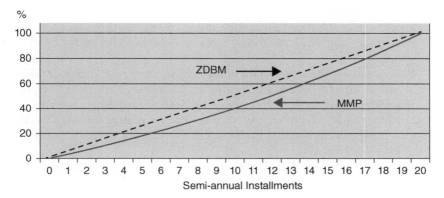

Figure 5.3 Rate of ownership transfer to the customer is less than pro rata in the MMP.

capital redemption until the completion of the contract. It is not pro rata – it does not meet the following condition at each time point:

$$\frac{\text{Proportion of loan returned}}{\text{Proportion of installments paid}} = 1 (\text{Proportion of loan retuned}$$
i.e. 1 – Proportion of loan outstanding).

The MMP does not meet the condition of the halfway results presented in Table 5.5.

In contrast, the ZDBM meets the requirement. Figure 5.3 brings out their schematic differences.

5.4.1 Relative efficiency

ZDBM has significant advantages over the MMP; the main ones are as follows.

1. ZDBM turns out to be cheaper for the customer because of faster capital redemption. Notice that in our illustration, the customer gains $ 21,108 – the difference between the columns E and F totals in Table 5.2

56 Financing consumer durables

2 Note that the customer does not gain at the cost of the bank – the sum of outstanding balances, the proxy for funding deposits, reduces proportionate to the contraction in aggregate return in both models.

Models Funding deposits Rqturnoncapital

$$\frac{ZDBN}{MMP} = \frac{840000}{947756} = \frac{33600}{37708} = 0.888^{\cdot}$$

Thus, the margin on funding deposits remains the same in both cases at 4%; ZDBM is a win-win structure for both parties. Islamic banks get an edge over their mainstream rivals. We return to this point later for its impact. In general, the model must increase liquidity in the financial system.

3 Researches show that constant amortization programs, such as ZDBM, are more equitable than others in use (Chambers et al. 2007). In our illustration, halfway on the time line, 50% ownership passes to the customer under the model as compared to 40% in the MMP. For the customer and the society, uniform amortization is equitable, uniform installments are not.

4 The MMP, like the ZDBM, also requires the creation of three contracts but of different character

   i   Creation of a joint ownership in property, with the bank and the customer being the partners
   ii The banker leases his share in the house to the customer on rent.

The customer undertakes to purchase units of the bank's share until ownership is fully transferred to him. Taken singly, the jurists regard the three transactions as valid if certain conditions are fulfilled. However, reservations abound about allowing their combination in a single contract. Scholars are particularly divided if the undertaking of the customer to buy back the bank's share in the property would be enforceable in a court of law in the absence of a consideration, if not for the lack of free will.

Under the scheme, the share units for buyback must differ; they cannot be uniform. Also, the mechanism of determining the fair value of each is missing. What is done is to treat the rent portion accruing to the customer as the market value of the share. The customer has no option but to agree to this dubious arrangement under the gaze of Shari'ah advisors to the bank.

5 In the case of default, the condition of the customer may be precarious in the MMP. Some banks have insisted that not only the balance of capital remaining unpaid but also the return on it for the remaining period must be allowable, as the bankers' have to meet on it their prior

commitment to depositors. In Malaysia, the law now grants relief to the hapless in such cases under a legal proviso.

6   The ZDBM is free of all the disabilities that afflict the MMP. Once a default takes place, the operation of the rental in the model comes to an end; the outstanding balance of capital alone is to be cleared. The ownership of the house is not in dispute, the property is freed of constructive liability once the outstanding amount is paid.

5.5 Concluding remarks

Our plea on the incompatibility of the MMP structure with Shari'ah norms of freedom from interest and pro rata transference of ownership to the customer in home financing started toward the close of 2008 and continued unabated until 2016. However, Islamic jurists did not take note of the blemishes of the MMP and continued endorsing contracts based on the compounding of returns on capital.

The jurists are seldom concerned about what mechanism banks use to arrive at uniform periodic payment installments. They enter into the picture only when the contract structure, with its terms and conditions, is presented to them for approval. This looks a bit oblique. We believe it is the duty of the experts to determine if the contract would remain lawful in operation.

The MMP structure is popular with bankers, as it brings them more money. Also, they feel at par with their mainstream rivals: they can follow their ways and imitate their products by just putting Islamic paint on them. The uniformity of installments is a big attraction both for bankers and their clients. However, it is easy to see that all uniform periodic payments in asset financing, including homes, that combine amortization and return on loan, no matter how determined, must result in compounding, and the asset ownership transfer to the customer must be less than the rate of amortization. Such payments are unlawful in Islam unless proven otherwise.

The ZDBM is free of compounding and fair to all stakeholders. It provides efficient service at minimal cost to all. Even conventional banks may use it for efficient performance to the benefit of themselves, their clients, and society at large. However, comments/suggestions for improving the model are most welcome.

5.6 Summary

- Islamic banks use the same tools as the mainstream to arrive at periodic installments – amortization of capital plus a return on it – the markup or rent. Mortgage-based loan contracts between the parties have to be certified by a competent panel of jurists as Shari'ah compliant.
- The MMP model uses equal periodic installments as those of the mainstream use; they also charge equal monthly installments – the EMIs.

58 Financing consumer durables

These installments combine part payment for the return of capital and part for the return on it like interest.

- However, the formula Islamic banks use to determine the installments is the same and compounds the return on capital. Thus, the MMP violates Islamic law.
- Compounding cannot be undone without making installments unequal.
- BBA is an offshoot of the MMP and has several variants across countries.
- Ownership of the house to the buyer in the MMP passes at a slower rate than the installment money. This is unjust and works against the buyer in case of a breach of contract.
- The ZDBM uses three contracts, including one based on constructive ownership. The installments are diminishing and free of compounding. The transfer of ownership to the buyer is pro rata.
- The ZDBM is more efficient than the MMP. It absorbs fewer funds, remaining no less beneficial to the parties than the MMP.

Chapter 6

Islamic financial markets character and instruments

Chapter contents

- Islamic financial markets:
- Money and capital market
- Direct and indirect modes
- Financial contracts and combined mode
- Murabahah, musharikah, ijara
- Salam, BBA, tawaruq, qard hasan

Preview

This chapter covers a large and significant area in Islamic finance, including money and capital markets, the nature of contracts used, and their types and the main instruments employed. It briefly examines their structuring, modus operandi, merits, and limitations. It focuses on murabahah, musharakah, and ijara and their variants. The treatment is essentially explanatory. No originality need be, sought as there is none except the diagrams used and the discussion on the markup issue.

6.1 Introduction

Financial markets are those where various types of securities are traded. They are of various types, including, but not restricted to, the markets for foreign exchange, money, stocks, and bonds. Financial markets are vital to the smooth operation of a capitalist society. Financial markets enable banks to borrow money and help them give loans to people wishing to borrow for various purposes. Islamic countries do need and have financial markets. These markets like others observe juridical norms and restrictions. They shun transactions involving interest, gharar, speculation, and other impermissible elements. They operate on participatory principles.

DOI: 10.4324/9781003366973-6

60 Islamic financial markets character and instruments

We restrict our discussion here to money and capital markets and the instruments they use. An instrument may have the same name but its structuring may be different. The literature on Islamic markets is voluminous and growing fast. There is no dearth of books, monographs, and articles on the subject. There exist comprehensive surveys of the growth of Islamic financial markets within Muslim countries and their global spread in competition with the interest-based mainstream markets in the normal run and during financial turmoil. There are numerous types of financial markets, but we restrict the discussion here to two: money and capital.

6.1.1 Money markets

The money markets are the providers of highly liquid, very safe, short-term debt securities. Because of these attributes, the securities are often seen as cash equivalents interchangeable for money at short notice.

These markets are vital for the smooth functioning of a modern financial economy. They allow savers to lend money to those in need of short-term credit and allocate funds toward their most productive uses. These loans often made overnight or for a matter of days or weeks are needed by governments, corporations, and banks in order to meet their near-term obligations or regulatory requirements. At the same time, it allows those with excess cash on hand to earn interest. The securities include short-term Treasuries (e.g., T-bills), certificates of deposit (CDs), commercial paper, repurchase agreements (repos), and money market mutual funds that invest in these instruments. The transaction tenure using these instruments ranges from overnight to 12 months, the commonest being less than or exactly three months.

The money markets are no less crucial for the smooth running of an Islamic economy than a secular one. It provides Islamic financial institutions with the facility for raising funds and adjusting portfolios over the short term. It enables Islamic banks to resolve their liquidity problems, specifically to handle the assets-liabilities mismatches. The central bank, in controlling the level of liquidity in the system, employs the money market for the transmission of its monetary policies. Governments and business organizations also find the money market useful for short-term investments and for raising short-term funds. Thus, it is indeed a venue where banks, businesses, and government can buy and sell money instruments and invest their surplus funds. Financial instruments and interbank investment allow surplus banks to channel funds to deficit banks, thereby maintaining the funding and liquidity balance.

The literature on the Islamic money market is scanty. It lacks substance and direction. It lacks short-term instruments, save for acceptance of debt or short-term deposits, essentially because Islam bans charging and accepting interest. Some jurists have of late ventured into putting Islamic garb on mainstream instruments like derivatives, futures, and options. Islamic banks in some places trade in these instruments. However, most Islamic banks are

Islamic financial markets character and instruments 61

free of this waywardness. Islamic finance is in dire need of developing legitimate short-term instruments.

6.1.2 Capital markets

All sorts of financial markets need capital for conducting their operations. They differ with reference to their objectives, the time dimension of their contracts, and the instruments they use. Money market transactions are of short duration, and their instruments are mostly what the economic activities generate. In contrast, capital market transactions are usually long term and are related more closely to the real economy. These markets bring together the businessmen who need money to invest in risky but lucrative ventures on the one hand and the money savers who carry surplus funds for their gainful utilization on the other. Capital markets provide them with a meeting place (Figure 6.1). They choose the instruments they agree to use. It is difficult to categorize these instruments. We divide them into direct and indirect modes.

6.1.3 Direct and indirect modes

In Chapter 5, we briefly stated the distinction usually made between the direct and indirect modes of financing Islamic banks use. The classification is generic and applications overlap. Still, the distinction helps us to understand the implications of the different modes and the same mode in different applications. To illustrate, *musharakah* is a direct mode when banks use it for financing a project in partnership with others because it is related directly to *value creation* in the production process. However, the same

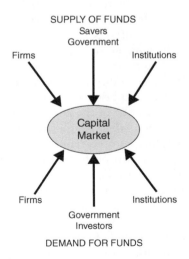

Figure 6.1 Capital Market Mediation.

62 Islamic financial markets character and instruments

mode becomes indirect if a bank uses it for acquiring part ownership of an existing asset with the stipulation that the client will purchase that part by paying periodic installments determined on a cost-plus basis. Indirect modes thus allow financing to facilitate the buying and selling of goods; no value added is involved. There is another example of this sort: Baqaras-Sadr is the lone exception in preferring another principle over the profit-and-loss sharing model for Islamic finance. He holds that financial intermediation could be provided on the principle of *jualah*, where the bank charges a specific fee for doing specific work for the client.

However, it is the cost-plus or markup sale or *murabahah* that takes center stage. Indeed, the mode has emerged as the leading species of a large genus. Most Islamic banks have a significant pool of *murabahah* receivables and exposure in either *ijarah* or declining balance partnership financings. In order to achieve liquidity, they are allowed under most *Shari'ah* rules to blend the receivables and the assets for sale to investment vehicles. In order to reduce their liquidity risks and to grow their businesses, most Islamic banks are actively engaged in product development and portfolio diversification in order to overcome the limitations of *murabahah* products. As there are interpretative variations in the explanations and usage of sale-related instruments, we shall keep close to the Governance Standards of the Accounting and Auditing Organization for Islamic Finance Institutions position in our discussion. We begin with a generic view of *murabahah*.

6.2 Murabahah

Murabahah is one of the most commonly used financing contracts in Islamic financing, albeit the question of whether *murabahah* defines Islamic requirements still lingers in the literature and shall be examined.

Candidly, *murabahah* falls in the same generic category of *uqud al-muawadhat* or exchange contracts that cover all types of transactions that Islam allows. In exchange contracts, a given quantity of one commodity is traded for a given quantity of *another* commodity, including money. The monetary value of a commodity is called its price. The delivery of a commodity and the payment of a price for it may be simultaneous – i.e., on the spot – or the obligation of one of the parties – buyer or seller – may be *deferred to* a future date. *Murabahah* belongs to the *deferred payment* contracts group. A client may, for example, request a bank to purchase a car for him on *murabahah* – i.e., cost-plus-profit basis, with the amount payable in monthly installments over a period of say five years. The arrangement *per se* does not contain any element of interest nor violate any other juristic norm. Islam does not grant a time value for money in contracts if *money were exchanged for the money*, which is the basis of banning interest. However, the markup in *murabahah* is allowed on the grounds that in Islam, "time has a share in price" (*lil zamani hazzunfi l thaman*). Indeed, it is this juristic pronouncement that constitutes the justification for allowing

Islamic financial markets character and instruments   63

the deferring of the payment obligation in Islamic contracts. Individually, *murabahah* contracts do not defy *Shari'ah* norms, but their overwhelming use over the years raises concern. This is because debt transactions dominate the scene at the cost of real economic promotion. To some, the use of *murabahah* contracts seems to have been overdone, and Islamic banks are advised at times to curb the leverage gain attraction that markup transactions tend to enlarge.

Some jurists feel that it is time to apply the principle of *saad-al-dharai* that closes the potential avenues for circumventing the *Shari'ah* norms, more so its objectives and spirit. It comes about that it is not the permissibility of *murabahah* contracts as such but their defective structuring and indiscreet use that tends to feed on the perception that Islamic banks are providing cover to the *murabahah* transaction. In actuality, the arrangement *per se* is entirely free of any such element. Home financing provides an interesting example of how *murabahah* use may go awry in structuring contracts.

6.2.1 The criticism

Even if we ignore the blemishes that creep into the MMP structure if the spreadsheet formula is used, the structure is not entirely free from difficulties. Some of the main weaknesses indicated in the literature are as follows.

1   There may arise and have arisen disputes in the MMP on the revision of the rental arrangement, the value of the property, and the amount of liability remaining unpaid once default takes place. In the conventional model, matters are clearer. Interest payment – the return on capital – stops at once in the case of default. The house will remain under charge for any outstanding balance of the loan plus interest on it until cleared.
2   The MMP also requires the creation of three transactions:

   a   The creation of a joint ownership agreement of the property.
   b   The bank/financier leases its share in the house to the customer through a rental agreement.
   c   The customer undertakes to purchase different units of the bank's share until the ownership is completely transferred to the customer. Taken singly, the jurists regard the three transactions as valid if certain conditions are fulfilled. However, their combination into a single contract is not allowed by some.

3   Scholars are divided on the issue of whether the undertaking of the customer to buy back the bank's share in the property would be enforceable in a court of law because of the absence of consideration, if not for the lack of free will.
4   The shares are not divided into uniform units, and the mechanism of determining the fair value of each is never in place. What is done is to

64 Islamic financial markets character and instruments

treat the rent portion accruing to the client as both the price and the market value of the share – customers never see a penny of the rent they earn. They have no option but to agree to this arrangement.

5   In the case of default, the position of the customer under the MMP may not be comfortable. A few banks have insisted that not only the balance of capital that remains outstanding but also the return on it for the remaining period must be treated as the unpaid liability of the client to meet the bank's commitment to their depositors. Some scholars provide implicit support for the MMP structure based on the argument that the interest rate serves only as a benchmark. This statement is misleading. A benchmark is the reference point to measure the efficacy of the actual value. If it is used in place of the value, it no longer remains a benchmark. As an analogy, sea level is used as the benchmark for measuring the heights of existing or future structures from the geographical viewpoint; it does not mean the construction begins at that level.

6.2.2 The markup issue

We have explained and illustrated the role of markup in *murabahah* financing, which is the backbone of modern Islamic banking. Still, the principle needs further clarification. In a *murabahah* sale, the markup principle is well understood but its incorporation in a purchase order requires a bit of explanation: AAOIFI Standard.

Standard No. 8 thus takes special care to lay down the rules for a purchase order in *murabahah* AAOIFI 2010: 151). Consider the case where Aamir shows a computer to Sohail and says, "Buy this for me and I will purchase it from you at cost plus 10%." Now, Imam Shafii is quoted as holding that the first transaction – Sohail buying the computer – would be valid, but Aamir, who made the promise to purchase it from Suhail has the right to withdraw his promise. If he does buy, it makes little difference if he pays the markup for the computer (cost plus 10%) immediately or at a later date. The example led to the evolution of the principle: sale with declared profit to the purchase order – i.e., markup is valid.

6.2.2.1 A guideline

Markups are among the main contributions to Islamic banks' earnings. However, it is not clear what guidelines decide the margins. Islamic banks are not monopolies, but the fact that they can fix markups implies that, like monopolies, they do have some pricing power. The resemblance can provide some guidance in the matter. Monopoly theory gives us a measure of pricing power based on the elasticity of demand. This formulation states the usual inverse relationship between the monopoly pricing power and the demand elasticity for his product.

Islamic financial markets character and instruments 65

$$\text{Price elasticity of demand } E = \frac{AR - MR}{AR}$$

In equilibriun price P = AR and MR = MC. Thus, we may write

$$E = \frac{P - MC}{P} \text{ This reduces to}$$

$$P = \frac{MC}{1 - \dfrac{1}{E}}$$

This formula is useful for fixing a just markup in *murabahah* if we know the marginal cost MC of producing a commodity at a given level of production and know or can estimate its price elasticity E. The upper limit of a markup can be fixed To illustrate, let us assume that the marginal cost of acquiring the watches is fixed at $44 and their elasticity of demand E = 5. Then a fair market price of the watches is likely to be: $55 apiece. Thus, the markup cannot be more than P – MC = $11 apiece, the maximum profit. The measure of course has limitations. The benefit of the markup to the financier/bank is the difference between the spot and deferred prices of the asset. The juristic legitimacy of this gain flows from the fact of the bank's ownership of the asset, the duration of the contract being immaterial and the risk involved being in line with the principle *al kharaj bi al daman*. Markup creates a predetermined fixed return on investment with little risk. So, it has become the dominant mode of financing with Islamic banks. Even conventional banks are lured to the instrument as the rate of interest is a controlled price while regulation of markups is yet to emerge.

6.3 The musharakah

The term *musharakah* is used in the Islamic mode of financing; it comes from the word *sharikah*, which means **sharing**. It can be separated into two types

6.3.1 Sharikat-ul-Milk

This refers to combined ownership of a property by two or more parties; it has two forms.

1 **Joint purchase:** The parties may jointly purchase, say, some machine. Joint ownership automatically results when heirs inherit the property of the deceased.
2 **Sharikat ul Aqd:** It means partnership by mutual contract. It has three subdivisions:
    (a) sharikat-ul-amaal, (b) sharikat-ul-amwaal, and (c) sharikat-ul-wajooh.

66   Islamic financial markets character and instruments

Some common features of the mode are as follows:

- A valid musharakah must meet all juridical requirements of a sale contract. All partners must contribute to investment capital.
- The contract must contain the profit-sharing ratios of the partners. According to Imam Malik and Shafi, profit is shared according to the percentage of investment. According to Imam Ahmad, the profit-sharing ratio can be different from investment. Imam Abu Hanifah attempts to reconcile both points of view. According to him, if a partner remains sleeping throughout the contract, the profit should not exceed his investment.
- On loss, all the Islamic jurists have one view that loss will be distributed according to the share of investment.
- Any partner can exercise his right to terminate the contract.
- If any of the partners dies or becomes insane, the contract automatically ends.

6.4 Other instruments

6.4.1 Leasing or ijarah

In principle, a person owning an asset, say a building, can give it on a lease (or rent) to another. However, in the context of financing, it is for a customer to request an institution, for example, a bank, to acquire an asset or to acquire the usufruct – the right to use it by paying rent. The institution can also execute a master agreement with the customer covering a number of *ijara* transactions that spell out the general terms and conditions of the agreement between the parties.

The institution may require customers to deposit a sum of money with it to guarantee their commitment to accepting a lease on the asset and the resulting obligations, with a view toward covering the damages, if any, that the institution suffers. *Ijara* can also operate in the reverse direction: customers can rent their property to the institution under a lease agreement. At face value, the leaser is earning a fixed income without taking any risk. The similarity with interest is seemingly striking. However, rent, unlike interest, is not a return on money. It is paid for by deriving a direct benefit from the use of a real asset. Furthermore, leasing is not entirely risk-free. The owner has to bear the cost of maintaining the asset in a usable condition throughout the lease period, which can be very long. Costs may arise for unforeseen causes and are likely to be uncertain. The magnitude and flow of benefits to the leaser may be below expectations. Thus, risk and uncertainty are present at both ends of the arrangement. Leasing or *ijara* is not financing *per se*; it only meets some of the requirements of leasing or rent.

Financing will come into the picture only when the leaser may want to own the asset for his use. Leasing may indirectly become the mode of financing. Consider the case where Furqaan approaches a bank to purchase a rentable asset, say a tourist bus. The bank may purchase the bus and give it to Furqaan on lease for good. The leasing of vehicles has been quite common in large towns with good transportation networks. Leasing is often combined with installment payments until the lessee eventually owns the asset. In such cases, the rental decreases with the payment of periodic installments. Home financing is a leading example of combining a lease with a sale. An important issue in the case of *ijara* is the right of the owner to sell the property to a third party before the expiry of the lease contract. The juristic position is that property rights allow the owner to sell the asset to anyone, even without informing the lessee. However, the latter will retain the right to use the property until the expiry of the usufruct that has materialized by virtue of the leasing contract. The seller becomes absolved of liability with the conclusion of the sale agreement. After the expiry of the lease, the new owner is free to renew or not renew the lease. This legal position has led to much litigation between owners – new and old – and lessees, creating social tensions. *Fiqhi* rulings have of late emerged to deal with such situations.

6.4.2 Hire purchase and rent sharing

One important variant of leasing that is used across countries but is more popular in Pakistan is the hire-purchase model. Under this mode of financing, the purchaser of an asset – i.e., the client – must know three things for sure: (i) the price of the asset, (ii) the profit margin of the bank in that price, and (iii) the amount of rent the client has to pay. After clearing the principal plus profit and rentals for the agreed period, the client becomes the owner of the asset. Some time back, the Islamic *Fiqh* Academy of the Organization for Islamic Cooperation (OIC) expressed the opinion that the use of the hire-purchase principle should be refrained unless adequate care is taken regarding the provision dealing with the extension of the lease period, the termination of the lease, the return of the asset to its owner, the purchase of the asset at the end of the contract, and so on. In the rent-sharing variant of leasing, the client pays in addition to the principal a specified share of the market rent of the asset, say a building, to the financier/bank until all payments have been made. Note that the bank's profit in the operation has to be incorporated into the agreed rentals.

6.4.3 Salam

Salam is a sale of a thing that is not available at the time of the conclusion of the sale but is to be delivered in the future on a specified date. However, the price for it has to be paid immediately after the contract is signed. The price – also referred to as the capital of *salam* – is to be paid in the form of money but can be in the form of fungible goods, including the usufruct of an asset, such as a building. In simple language, *salam* refers to the sale of a determinate thing for an agreed price immediately payable with the delivery of the asset at a future date. The sanction follows from the Qur'an: "*O you who believe! When you deal with each other in transaction involving future obligation for a fixed period reduce them into writing*" (2:282).

Salam finds support from traditions as well. For example, Ibn Abbas narrated that when the Prophet (peace be upon him), on arrival in Medina, found merchants practicing forward sales (i.e., *salam*) in fruits for one or two years in advance. He declared, "[A]nyone who pays money in advance for dates (to be delivered later) should pay it for a specified measure or a specified weight and a specified period" (Bukhari sahih, III, PP. 234–44, *Ahadith* 441 and 443). The application of *salam* is regarded as being more appropriate for forward trading in the areas of agriculture and natural resources.

6.4.3.1 Parallel salam

In the aforementioned case, it is permissible for the buyer – say the client of a bank – to enter into an agreement with a farmer. Here, the bank becomes the seller of *salam* for acquiring goods similar to the specifications recorded in the first *salam* contract. This arrangement is technically known as *parallel salam*. In Figure 6.2, C is a seller while the remaining three entities A, B, and D act either as a buyer or as a seller depending upon the nature of the contract each enters into. Thus, in the original *salam* contract (1), A is the buyer of the commodity and B is the seller. The remaining four contracts are each a case of parallel *salam* arising out (1). For example, A can sell forward the commodity to a trader D (contract 2). A can also be a buyer of a *salam* from D (now a bank) to make spot payment B (contract 4). This can be a *murabahah* contract with a markup operating on the ZDBM pattern, as discussed in the context of home financing earlier. In this way, A can avoid parking his own money with B for the entire duration of the original

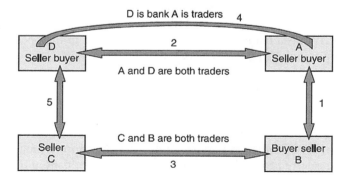

Figure 6.2 Salam and parallel *salam* operations.

salam (1). The bank can cover itself for delivery by entering into a purchase contract with a seller like C (contract 5).

6.4.4 Istisna'

Istisna' is a contract of exchange with deferred delivery. It is applicable to the making or constructing of ordered items. The mode is based on a reported request of the Prophet (peace be upon him) to have a pulpit and a finger ring made for him. Another basis is the promotion of social welfare through the expansion of public utilities. Interestingly, even though there is a lack of general agreement on the operational conditions for *istisna'*, a few requirements are insisted upon. These include the following:

- The item to be delivered must be clearly specified in terms of its nature, quality, and measurements.
- The manufacturer (builder) must make a commitment to produce the item as per the description and specifications.
- The manufacturer (builder) is to deliver the item upon the completion of its production without needing a fixed completion date.
- The contract cannot be revoked once the production process has started except where items are found to be not meeting the specifications as per the agreement.
- The payment can be made in installments linked with the progress of the work or in a lump sum before or after the time of delivery.
- The manufacturer (builder) alone is responsible for obtaining the inputs needed for the completion of the production process.
- The manufacturer (builder) cannot assume the role of a financial intermediary between the buyer and the third party, especially if the buyer has become unable to meet the obligations toward such a third party. Figure 6.3 helps explain the operation of *istisna'* in a typical manufacturing contract.

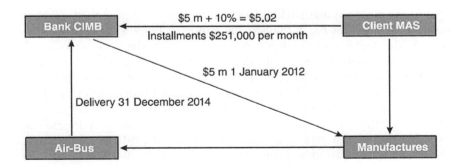

Figure 6.3 Istisna' in operation.

6.5 Combining the modes

On the operational side, banks mostly combine two or more financing modes to make a package – i.e., a product salable to their clients. We have already observed such combining in the discussion on home financing, for example. Jurists have framed some rules for transactions that comprise more than one contract combined in one set. AAOIFI Standard No. 25 (AAOIFI 2010: 441–459) spells out these rules for guidance in this matter. In brief, the main points are as follows:

- Combining should not include the cases that *Shari'ah* explicitly bars. For example, a sale and lending cannot be part of the same set.
- The combination cannot be used as a trick to introduce *riba* by the back door, for example, when two parties may practice *bai'inah* even though it is allowed in Malaysia under restrictions.
- Combining should not be used as an excuse for *riba* taking. For example, A buys a book from B for $100 today on the promise that B will buy back the book for $120 a year later. The literature quotes such cases from the thirteenth-century practices in the Muslim lands.
- Combined contracts should not reveal a disparity or contradiction with regard to their underlying rulings and ultimate goals. Examples of contradictory contracts include granting an asset to someone as a gift and selling or leasing it to the person simultaneously.

These explanations are only illustrative, not exhaustive. Indeed, there can be innumerable permutations and combinations of contracts, so it is important that each individual case is scrutinized for its validity. This has given rise to divergences in juridical decisions and has added to the *Shari'ah* risks in Islamic finance. There is, in particular, one set of combinations that merits further discussion: the BBA structure.

6.5.1 The BBA structure

One of the most popular packages of Islamic finance to meet the long-term needs of clients is the *bai bi thaman ajil*, popularly known as the BBA structure. As the Arabic name makes explicit, under BBA, the bank offers to sell to clients the assets they need on a deferred payment basis. The bank makes a cash payment to the seller of the product that the client needs to purchase and becomes its owner. The client then buys that product from the bank immediately on a cost-plus contract. The client pays the cost-plus amount in equal installments over the contract period. The plus factor is determined by using the interest rate as a benchmark. However, BBA is a sale where the return is considered as profit. Figure 6.4 outlines the structure in the

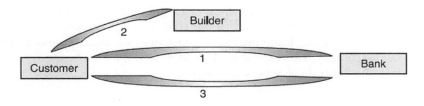

Figure 6.4 The BBA structure.

case of a house purchase between the builder, the customer, and the bank. The sequence of contracts in BBA, using the purchase of a house as an example, is as follows:

1. The customer identifies a house he wants to purchase and approaches the bank for the necessary financing. The bank agrees.
2. The customer buys the house from the builder and pays in full using bank financing, but, as per the agreement, he immediately sells the property to the bank at the purchase price, which is equivalent to the financing provided by the bank.
3. The customer then buys back the same house from the bank at a marked-up selling price, which the customer has to pay in uniform periodic installments. BBA dominated home financing arrangements in Malaysia for over two decades, but then it was found that the banks' buyback (*inah*) contract in the package was of doubtful validity. It was argued that in BBA, the bank operated as a mere financier rather than as a property vendor. And in the case of a customer's inability to continue paying the installments, the insistence of banks not to forego the unpaid profit part, taking back only the remaining capital, led to the mode falling into disrepute. Even though most jurists do not regard *inah* as permissible, Malaysia and Brunei continue to use it in the BBA home financing model on the basis of the interpretative divergence that Islam allows and because local jurists approve of it.

However, the use of *inah* has to meet the conditions that the Shai'i school of jurisprudence requires and the commodity involved must be *non-ribawi*. Despite these allowances, BBA is on the way out; banks are fast giving up the mode in favor of the MMP model discussed earlier.

6.5.2 Tawarruq

Tawarruq in Islamic finance is a somewhat controversial instrument used to generate cash for the borrower. He purchases an item from the bank on deferred payment – i.e., a cost-plus basis – but sells it back immediately to the bank at cost price to obtain the needed cash. The reservation is that the transactions add nothing real to the economy; the markup paid and received is interest that Islam prohibits. *Tawarruq* increases the amount of debt in an economy. However, it is allowed in Malaysia under the facility principle. We illustrate next how it works.

6.5.2.1 Illustration 1

Aamir & Co. is a sound firm, but due to a slower realization of their receivables, they fall critically short of cash to run business operations smoothly and approach their bank to provide them with liquidity (RM100, 000) to overcome the difficulty. The bank offers the company a contract to buy a building for RM100,000 and to sell it to the company in installments with a 12% markup. The company sells the building to a third party (Ahmad) for cash at cost price. See Figure 6.4 for a diagrammatic representation of this arrangement.

6.5.2.2 Illustration 2

Ashraf is willing to have a one-year investment deposit worth PKR1 million with Meezan Bank but wants a sure return of 12% for the year. The bank buys a machine from Ashraf for PKR1,000,000 + 12% = 1,120,000, payable in monthly installments, but sells the machine back to him for PKR 1,000,000. Ashraf leaves the money with the bank as a one-year investment deposit. By the end of the year, Ashraf gets back his money with a 12% return (see Figure 6.5 for a diagrammatic representation of this arrangement). Juridical opinion on the validity of such transactions is much divided. We will not comment further on this topic here but will leave students to debate the issue.

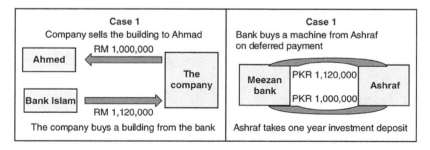

Figure 6.5 The two uses of tawaruq.

Islamic financial markets character and instruments   73

6.6 Benevolent loan (*qard hasan*)

As Islam prohibits interest on all sorts of loans, a loan, by definition, can only be free of charge – i.e., a benevolent loan. It is granted on the grounds of compassion and to help a fellow Muslim in dire need. The Prophet (peace be upon him) advocated fervently for the grant of such loans to those in distress. Several traditions eulogize this sort of lending:

6.7 Summary

The chapter carried forward the preceding discussion in Chapter 5 on Islamic modes of financing. It explained and illustrated the indirect financing instruments, which essentially are sale based.

- In *murabahah*, one commodity is traded for another commodity, including money, No addition to the price is allowed in spot transactions. However, time assumes a value in deferred payment pricing in the form of markups.
- Marked-up or cost-plus pricing currently dominates Islamic finance. This dominance has raised alarm in some quarters, including the central banks of some countries.
- There are no systemic and agreed guidelines for fixing the markups. However, markups can be derived from the monopolistic pricing theory, in which elasticity of demand is the essential influence in determining the markup: it must vary inversely with the price elasticity of the product.
- The owner of an asset, say a building or a piece of land, can lease it out to another economic entity. Renting (*ijara*) to earn an income is a common practice in modern societies.
- *Salam* involves the sale of something which is not in existence or possession of the seller. In this respect, it is an exception to the general requirement. In *salam*, the agreed price has to be paid promptly; the delivery is to be made in the future, but the date of delivery is not specified. An initial *salam* contract may give rise to multiple parallel *salam* contracts.
- *Istisna'* is a contract applicable to made-to-order items for future delivery. There is no general agreement among the jurists on rules regulating the contract, although some guidelines are available in the literature. Like *salam*, there are also parallel *istisna'* contracts.
- *Tawarruq* is an instrument that Islamic banks (especially in Malaysia) use to provide liquidity(cash) to clients to meet a temporary shortage of funds. It may also be used to ensure a fixed return over a certain period to investment depositors. In either case, the cash available to the client is less than what the client has to pay in purely financial transactions. *Tawarruq* is said to increase the volume of debt in an economy.

- As Islam prohibits interest, cash loans can only be advanced free of cost. Islam encourages such benevolent lending (*qard hasan*) to help people in financial distress. The reward for such a loan in the hereafter is greater than charity, as per Prophetic traditions, but the loan has to be paid back unless the lender grants a waiver.

Chapter 7

Investment sukuk
Islamic bonds

Chapter contents

- Meaning, structure, and significance
- Sukuk, equity, and conventional bonds
- The variants and their combinations
- Structuring and underlying contracts
- Murabahah, musharakah, ijara, others
- Sukuk markets expansion and problems

This chapter discusses an important instrument used in Islamic financial markets called *sukuk*. It has many characteristics of conventional bonds to the extent that it is at times referred to as the Islamic bond but the two are not the same even as sukuk, like conventional bonds, carry one or more of the risks relating to credit, rate of return, price, liquidity. Still, sukuk are different as they shun interest and follow other Islamic restrictions. Their structuring is based on Islamic modes like *shirka*, *mudarabah*, and *ijara*. Sukuk has fast gained popularity not only in Muslim lands but across Western countries as well. Sukuk is found to have an edge over interest-based conventional bonds on several counts and has emerged as a viable alternative.

7.1 Introduction

7.1.1 Meaning and origin

Similar to the Western bond, sukuk is the Arabic name for a financial certificate that conforms to Islamic strictures on interest. '*Sukuk*' is the plural form of the word '*sakk*', but is now used in a singular sense as well. The issuer of sukuk must also make a contractual commitment to buy back

DOI: 10.4324/9781003366973-7

76 Investment sukuk

the bond on a future date at par value. Sukuk securities are designed to pay profit generally linking the investment to some tangible asset. The term was first used for papers representing financial obligations originating from trade and other commercial activities in the Islamic premodern period. The first sukuk transaction reportedly took place in Damascus in its Great Mosque in the 7th century AD.

The coverage and forms of sukuk have since changed. Their present structuring is different from the early *sukuk*. Today, there is a replication of conventional securitization. The process of preparing salable certificates is backed by real assets. Securitization transfers the ownership of underlying assets to the *sukuk* holders, and the certificates represent a proportionate value of the *jointly* held assets.

Sukuk put Islamic institutions on par with the conventional in terms of their trappings. This helps them stand in competition with their conventional rivals in the global markets earning, in the process, the title of 'Islamic bonds'. *Sukuk* have the strategy of embedding a trade element in the product design so that the settlement of cash could be made on a deferred basis. The technique enables the outcome of financing transactions to become allowable Islamic debt. The fact that around 80% of Islamic financing is currently no more than commercial debt is evidence of the policy's success. *Sukuk have become* a systemic imperative.

7.1.2 Differences

Despite similarities, sukuk are much different from conventional bonds. A conventional bond is a debt instrument that represents a sum of money that a legal entity borrows from a lender on a fixed rate of interest for a specified period of time. This rate of interest is also called the coupon rate. Bonds are fixed-income securities. They may be issued by private-sector companies or public authorities – national or international – to finance different sorts of projects and activities. Bonds are one of the three main asset classes traded in financial markets, the other two being stocks and cash equivalents.

The borrower is called the issuer of the bond and the lender the investor. The interest is usually paid half-yearly, and the principal is to be returned on maturity. Before maturity, bonds can be bought and sold at discounted values. Credit quality and duration are the two main features of a bond that plays a major role among the determinants of its coupon rate. Bond maturities range from a 90-day Treasury bill to a 30-year government bond; corporate issues stand midway and are often of 10-year durations.

In contrast, Islam prohibits the giving and taking of interest. Therefore, the approach in designing *sukuk* has been no different from the case of most Islamic finance instruments. Taking the conventional bond structure, the interest rate is removed, and the contract is wrapped around an asset base involving a deferred payment so that it meets the *Shari'ah* requirements. We shall soon discuss the ways of accomplishing this task. For now, let us identify the main features of *sukuk* as they are described in Standard No. 17 of the Accounting and Auditing Organization for Islamic Financial Institutions (AAOIFI, 2010). The description uses the term "investment *sukuk*", presumably for the following reasons:

1. Investment *sukuk* are certificates of equal value representing either shares in the ownership of undivided tangible assets or usufruct – i.e., the right to use the assets, to get the services out of the assets, such as a house, for example. They may also refer to the ownership of shares in the assets of particular projects or of some special investment activity.
2. However, this view of *sukuk* will be applicable only (a) after the value of the *sukuk* subscribed for has been received from the investors and the subscription has been closed, and (b) the funds received have actually been employed in achieving the purpose they were raised to finance. Provision 2(b) requires further clarification because undue delay in starting to use the fund may work against the interest of the investors in terms of the flow of earnings.

To illustrate how *sukuk* are employed for different purposes, let us take the case of lease-ownership certificates. The developer of a residential complex, who deals in selling houses, arranges the funds for a project from a financial intermediary, say a banker, authorizing him to issue *sukuk* certificates for public subscription to recover his investment. The *sukuk* certificates embody lease contracts that eventually make the holders homeowners. Alternatively, the objective of the developer may not be to sell the houses but to keep them as rentals as a source of future income. In that case, the bank may have an agreed share in the rentals. The setup can be used in the case of existing assets or for those created in the future.

7.2 Bonds, equity shares, and *sukuk*

Conventional bonds and equity shares have long been the sources of obtaining investment funds; *sukuk* are recent additions. The three instruments are now used by public-sector and private-sector organizations for fundraising to finance their projects. It is necessary to know their distinctive features in order to understand the role of each in modern finance. This is even more important because *sukuk* are often criticized for replicating conventional bonds. Admittedly, the two have similarities, but they are also different in important ways.

A bond is a debt contract that requires the issuer (debtor) to pay to each *individual* bondholder the principal amount plus interest on a specified date. As such, the bondholders are interested in the assets of the issuer company because their capital and interest are tied up in the issuer company. In contrast, *sukuk* holders have beneficial ownership in the common *pool* of assets underlying the issue. They are entitled to a share in the revenues generated by such assets but not in their value until the assets are liquidated and the proceeds are distributed. They have a stake in the operational results of the company. A bondholder is free to sell the certificate at any time in the bond market for cash at the current price. Such liberty is not available to a *sukuk* debt base unless *sukuk* do not represent pure debt but are a mixed portfolio of debt and tangible assets. Even though the *sukuk* certificate too is a realizable debt, the holder cannot trade it in the secondary market except at par value. Instead, the *sukuk* holder has to retain the certificate until maturity.

Not necessarily related to a declared purpose, the issuer of bonds is free to use the funds raised in any way it deems fit. In contrast, *sukuk* funds cannot be utilized independently of the purpose for which they are issued. *Sukuk* issuance has most commonly been project-specific, asset-specific, and balance-sheet specific. A brief explanation of each follows:

a   *Project-specific sukuk*: In this category falls the *sukuk* issued to finance a particular project. For instance, Qatar issued *sukuk* in 2003 to raise funds for the construction of Hamad Medical City (HMC) in Doha. A joint-venture 'special purpose vehicle' (SPV) (see the following), the Qatar Global *Sukuk*, was incorporated with limited liability for acquiring land. This land was registered in the name of the HMC Trust, which issued *sukuk* certificates worth US$700 million, payable by October 2010, at the annual floating rate defined as Libor + 0.45%.

b   *Asset-specific sukuk*: In this case, the beneficiary rights of assets are sold to the investors. Two examples are of interest for noting the structuring difference. The Government of Malaysia collected US$600 million in 2002 through *sukuk* issuance. The arrangement included a land sale of beneficiary rights to an SPV, which then resold the rights to investors for five years. Bahrain issued *sukuk* for US$250 million payable in five years to finance the extension of their airport. *Sukuk* trust certificates in both cases were based on *ijarah* or leasing contracts, but there was a difference. In Malaysia, the SPV was an intermediary between the government and the investors, while in Bahrain, the land was leased directly to investors. Also, the Bahrain issue was a mixture based on a purpose-asset combination.

c   *Balance-sheet-specific sukuk*: The *sukuk* issuance by the Islamic Development Bank (IDB) in August 2003, due for maturity in 2008, was intended to mobilize US$400 million from the international market for augmenting its resources to finance various projects in member countries. It is a good example of the balance-sheet-specific use of the instrument

Sukuk certificates are also different from equity certificates. Equity stocks are issued by corporate bodies to be used as a general financial base normally covering the cost of a fixed asset and a part of working capital.

Equities carry no guaranteed returns and are traded on the stock market. One may or may not get a favorable return in the end. In contrast, bonds involve lending money to the company at a fixed interest rate so, at the end of everything, one is able to calculate the amount one receives in return after a certain period of time. As such, bonds carry lesser risk, but one has to lend out more for comparable earnings. Thus, *sukuk* are like bonds, although they are, as we saw, of a different sort. They are also less risky than equity shares.

7.2.1 Structuring the sukuk

Structuring the *sukuk* is a complex process and involves intricate decision-making. The purpose of issuance, the type of contract to be used, the amount of return and maturity issues, the sort SPV to be created and the risk involved all have to be considered. The juridical implications of various decisions are the most vulnerable part of the entire structuring process. For this reason, *sukuk* are categorized with reference to the Islamic contract employed in their structuring. We follow this categorization in the discussion in the next section.

7.2.2 Mudarabah sukuk

Sukuk in this case are project-specific investments and represent equal-value units in *mudarabah* assets. The *sukuk* units one owns are registered like equity in the holder's name. The investors share the returns from the undivided asset pool proportionate to the number of units each holds. The contract is based on the official prospectus that must provide all relevant information in order to be *Shari'ah* compliant, for example, the nature of the capital, profit-sharing ratios (PSRs), and other conditions related to the issue. The *mudarabah sukuk* (MS) holders are entitled to transfer the ownership of the *sukuk* by selling the certificate in the securities market at their discretion, subject to the following provisions:

A   If the project has not started and *mudarabah* capital is still in the form of money, trading or transfer of the MS can only be at par value.
B   If capital is in the form of a combination of cash, receivables, goods, real assets, and benefits, trade must be based on market price by mutual agreement.
C   The *mudarib* (entrepreneurs) who have collected a fund from the subscribers to the MS can invest their own funds too, creating a mixed model. They will receive profit for their capital contribution in addition to their share in the profit as *mudarib*.
D   The issuer or the fund manager should not give any guarantee for the capital or of a fixed return on capital or on any portion of it. The profit – not the revenue or the yield – must be divided in accordance

80 Investment sukuk

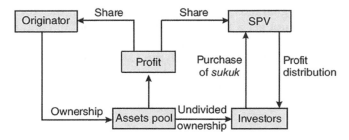

Figure 7.1 General structure of mudarabah-based sukuk.

    with *Shari'ah* rules. Also, the profit and loss account of the project should be published and made available to the MS holders.

E   The creation of reserves out of the profit for contingencies, such as the loss of capital, is allowed. The promise by a third party external to the MS contract to donate a specific sum without any counter-benefit to meet losses in the given project can be included in the prospectus. *Mudarabah*-based *sukuk* have some structural variations. Figure 7.1 depicts their general form.

7.2.2.1 Illustration 1

Shamil Bank of Bahrain raised investment funds worth Saudi riyal 360 million through the Al Ehsa Special Realty *mudarabah*. The bank used the amount for investment participation in a land development transaction with a Saudi real estate development company with the objective of having a share in the annual returns arising from participating in the financing of the *mudarabah* project. Profits accrue to the bank from the share in returns on its share in *mudarabah* investment.

7.2.3 Musharakah sukuk

Musharakah sukuk is used for mobilizing funds for establishing a new project or developing an existing one or financing a business activity on the basis of partnership contracts. The certificate holders become the owners of the project or the assets of the activity as per their respective shares. These *musharakah* certificates can be treated as negotiable instruments and can be bought and sold in the secondary market. They act like corporate equity and in structure they resemble MS, except that they are in the form of a relationship between their issuers and the holders. Unlike MS, the issuer of the *sukuk* forms a committee, which includes *sukuk* holders among its members. According to AAOIFI guidance, this committee can be

Investment sukuk 81

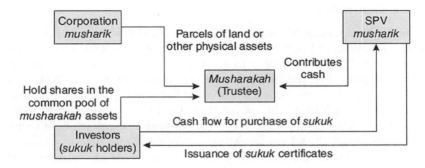

Figure 7.2 Operational structure of musharakah sukuk.

consulted regarding investment decisions. As in MS, the certificates here are also of equal value. Funds are raised with the intention of using the funds to launch a new project, to expand or renovate an existing facility, or to finance some business activity on the basis of a contractual partnership such that the *sukuk* holders become the owners of the project or the assets involved in the activity, proportionate to their holdings. According to AAOIFI Standards, the *musharakah* certificates can be managed on the principle of participation using the *musharakah*, *Mudarabah*, or agency structure. They are also tradable in the secondary market. The corporation undertaking the project and the *sukuk* issuer agree to the creation of what is called an SPV to work as an intermediary between the parties as a trustee. The SPV enters into a *musharakah* arrangement with the project-owner corporation for a fixed period of time on the basis of an agreed PSR. The corporation undertakes to buy the *musharakah sukuk* certificates of the SPV, which it issues on behalf of the investors, on a periodic basis (see Figure 7.2).

7.2.3.1 Illustration 2

In 2005, Dubai Islamic Bank (DIB), acting for the United Arab Emirates, successfully launched the world's first airline *sukuk* bond worth US$550 million to finance the development of Emirates' new engineering center and Emirates Group headquarters. The deal was a joint effort of a prestigious consortium of local, regional and international banks, led by the DIB. The issue was managed by a six-member group of banks, including the DIB, the National Bank of Abu Dhabi, the Gulf International Bank BSC, the Standard Chartered Bank, HSBC, and UBS. The *sukuk* managed to attract wide investor participation from Europe, as well as from the Far East.

82 Investment sukuk

7.2.3.2 Illustration 3

In 2002, Sitara Chemical Industries Ltd floated a public issue of their term finance certificates (TFCs) worth PKR340 million, based on a profit-and-loss-sharing (PLS) arrangement to augment the project financing capacity of the company. The certificates were fully subscribed by June 2002. The maturity term of the certificates was fixed at five years. The PLS was applied to the operating profits of the *musharakah*. The project resulted in a loss for the parties. It was a simple case of *musharakah sukuk* involving no intermediaries. *Musharakah* and *mudarabah* are quite similar. In both cases, *sukuk* holders share profit and loss with the project operator (or entrepreneur). The difference is that in *musharakah*, all participants are insiders as shareholders in the corporation.

In contrast, *sukuk* holders under *mudarabah* are external suppliers of funds – they normally cannot participate in the decision-making or managerial aspects of the business. Thus, the agency factor makes capital costs relatively higher under *mudarabah*.

7.2.4 Ijara sukuk

According to AAOIFI Standards, these are *sukuk* that represent the ownership of equal shares in real estate or in the usufruct of the real estate. They are securities that give their owners the right to own the well-defined real estate that is tied into a lease contract. The *sukuk* holders receive the rent and can dispose of their certificates in a manner that does not affect the right of the lessee, i.e. the certificates are tradable. The holders of such *sukuk* bear all the costs of maintenance of, and the repairing of damage to, the real estate. In other words, expenses related to the corpus or basic characteristics of the assets are the responsibility of the owner, while maintenance expenses related to its operation are to be borne by the lessee. The payment of *ijara* rentals must be unrelated to the period of usufruct undertaken by the lessee. It can be made before the beginning of the lease period, during the period, or after the period, subject to the circumstances of the case and by the mutual agreement of the parties. This flexibility can be used to evolve different forms of contract and *sukuk* that may serve different purposes for the issuers and the holders. For an *ijara* contract, it is necessary that the assets being leased – whether existing or to be constructed – and also its rental are clearly known to the parties at the time of entering the contract.

The leaser should normally be able to acquire, construct, or buy the asset being leased by the time set for its delivery to the lessee (AAOIFI 2010: 140–157). The leaser can sell the leased asset to a third party provided it does not hinder the lessee in taking benefit from the asset. The new owner would be entitled to receive the rentals. The procedure for the issuance of *ijara sukuk* envisages the creation of an SPV that issues *sukuk* to the

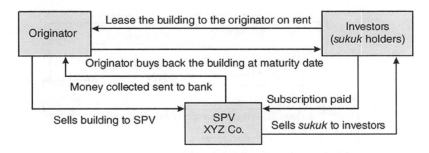

Figure 7.3 Common structure of ijara sukuk.

investors to mobilize funds for purchasing the asset(s) on their behalf from the originator. The asset is then leased back to the originator for use. The lessee makes periodic rental payments to the SPV that in turn distributes the same to the *sukuk* holders. Figure 7.3 outlines the essential steps involved in the structuring of *ijara sukuk*.

Ijara sukuk are popular as they offer a high degree of flexibility in matters of issuance management and marketability. The central government, municipalities, *awqaf* (endowment), or any other asset users, private or public, can issue these *sukuk*. Additionally, they can be issued by financial intermediaries or directly by users of the leased assets, as in Illustration 3.

7.2.5 Murabahah sukuk

These are one of the three types of *sukuk* that are characterized as debt-based; the other two are those based on *istisna'* and *tawarruq*. Here the issuer of certificates is the seller of some specified commodity, say, a fleet of passenger buses. The funds that the subscribers contribute are used to pay for the agreed cost of the fleet. The certificate holders become the owners of the commodity and are entitled to the revenue generated from its final sale to the users. They, *ipso facto*, hold certificates of debt advanced to the issuer against future delivery of the commodity. For this reason, *sukuk* generated mainly on a *mudarabah* basis in the primary market are not negotiable instruments or tradable in the secondary markets *save at their par value*. Charging a different price would amount to trading in debt. There are three variations of *sukuk* involving *murabahah* as the basis of their issuance. These may be described as follows:

- An actual sale and purchase of an asset involving three parties where the asset moves directly between the seller and the buyer.
- A sale and buyback of the same commodity or *bai-al-inah*, with prior agreement between two parties.
- A tripartite agreement involving agency sale operations – i.e., *tawarruq*.

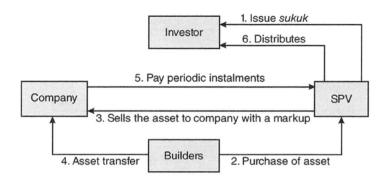

Figure 7.4 Structure of murabahah sukuk.

Figure 7.4 sketches the structuring process of *sukuk* for acquiring an asset, say, a building.

These variants of *murabahah sukuk* have been in use in Malaysia since 2000 for term financing. They were also tradable in domestic financial markets. However, of late, these *sukuk* are being phased out and participatory structures such as *musharakah*, *mudarabah*, and *ijara* are rapidly substituting them.

7.2.5.1 Illustration 4

Although *murabahah sukuk* are now being phased out, we have an interesting example of their use from Kazakhstan. A local bank, the BTA, took the initiative of introducing Islamic finance in the country with agency-based commodity *murabahah* in July 2007 for agency work that was given to a group that comprised two Abu Dhabi banks – Islamic and commercial – Barclays Capital and the CIMB from Malaysia. The Abu Dhabi Islamic Bank (ADIB) was to lead the agency. Instead of issuing certificates, the agency struck a deal syndicating 14 financiers from Europe, the Middle East, and Malaysia. The BTA sought funding for financing trade activities observant of Islamic norms. The funding was initially launched to raise US$150 million but was later extended to US$250 million in view of oversubscription. Figure 7.5 sketches the bare structure of this rather complicated arrangement.

7.2.6 Salam sukuk

Salam sukuk are certificates of equal value that a producer of a certain fungible commodity – whether tangible or intangible – issues for the purpose of mobilizing resources so that the producer can supply the contracted goods for delivery in the future to the certificate holders. To clarify, the issuer of the certificates is a seller of the goods of *salam*, and the subscribers are the buyers of those goods. On completion of the contract, the *salam* certificate

Investment sukuk 85

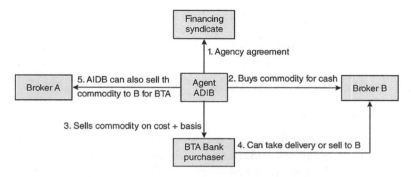

Figure 7.5 The use of murabahah sukuk in Kazakhstan.

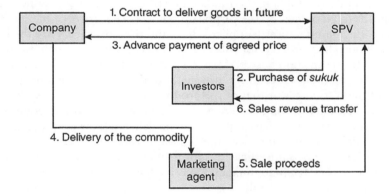

Figure 7.6 General structure of slum.

holders become owners of the goods and are entitled to the revenue either from the sale of certificates in the market or the sale price of the goods sold through a parallel *salam*, if there is one. Thus, the recovery of their investment is arranged.

Salam sukuk are dynamic instruments used to raise funds for a variety of purposes from the acquisition of fixed assets to augmenting working capital. Originating in agriculture, their use was extended to all sorts of economic activities, including manufacturing and trading. In Sudan, agricultural producers used them, and in Bahrain in 2001, the Central Bank of Bahrain used them to raise funds for the aluminum industry. Figure 7.6 illustrates the general structuring of *salam sukuk*.

All the standard Shari'ah requirements that apply to salam also apply to salam sukuk, such as full payment by the buyer at the time of contracting the sale; the standardized nature of the underlying asset; the clear enumeration of quantity, quality, date, and place of delivery of the asset; and the purchased goods cannot be resold before actual possession is obtained at the maturity of the contract because that would amount to the selling of debt. The restriction makes the instrument nonliquid and to that extent, it is less attractive. Investors would therefore be more inclined to buy *salam sukuk* if they expect the prices of the underlying goods to rise by the maturity date.

7.2.7 Istisna' sukuk

Salam and *istisna'* look identical as modes of financing. *Salam* originated in the pastoral era of history, and thus the traditional source of *salam* confined the contract to the raising of resources for cultivation. When the mode is extended to manufacturing, the notion of *istisna'* derives from the *salam* rules. *Istisna' sukuk* are certificates that carry equal value and are issued with the aim of mobilizing the funds required for producing products that are meant to be owned by the certificate holders. The issuer of these certificates is the manufacturer (supplier/seller) and the subscribers are the buyers of the product ordered for future delivery. The *sukuk* contributions are intended to pay the purchase price of the product in advance. The certificate holders, being the owners of the product, are therefore entitled to the sale price of the certificates or that of the product. The product can also be sold through a parallel *istisna'*, if there is one. The typical terms and conditions of an *istisna'* contract specify the assets to be delivered, the price details, the expected delivery time, and any other relevant facts.

Istisna' sukuk are quite efficacious for financing large infrastructural projects because they facilitate financial intermediation by permitting the producer/seller to have parallel *istisna'* – i.e., there is discretion for sub-contractors to help meet the order. To illustrate, a financial institution may undertake the construction of a facility for deferred payment, employing a specialist firm to do the actual work. Figure 7.7 exhibits the basic

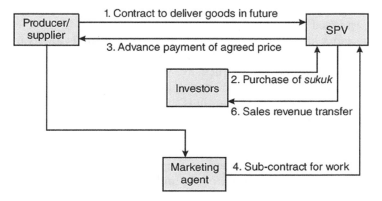

Figure 7.7 Structure and contract sequence of istasna sukuk.

structure of *istisna' sukuk* and the sequence of steps involved. *Istisna' sukuk*, being debt-based, cannot be sold to a third party at any price other than their face value; clearly, then, the certificates cannot be traded in the secondary market.

7.2.7.1 Illustration 5

On 23 June 2008, Malaysian Southern Link Berhad (MSLB) issued *istisna' sukuk* worth RM900 million and with 18–20 years' maturity using the *bai-al-inah* mode to develop, operate and maintain the Eastern Dispersal Link in Johar Bahru, which was deemed to be the *istisna'* asset. CIMB worked as the trustee for the investors. MSLB (the issuer) entered into a contract with CIMB (the trustee), agreeing to construct and deliver the link to the bank that bought the link, paying its *spot* price to MSLB. The bank then entered into a contract with the same company – i.e., MSLB – selling back to it the asset – the link that it had bought in the first contract – at cost plus the agreed profit. MSLB then issues *istisna' sukuk* to investors through the CIMB to meet its obligations to the bank under the sale contract.

7.2.7.2 Illustration 6

Five-year global corporate *istisna' sukuk* were issued by Tabreed on behalf of the National Central Cooling Company, with the United Arab Emirates providing a fixed coupon of 5.5%. The funds were needed to redeem an existing debt worth around US$136 million. The *sukuk* structure was very complicated and involved a combination of *ijara*, *istisna'* and *ijarah-mawsufahfi-al dhimmah* (or forward leasing contracts). Figure 7.8 shows their structuring.

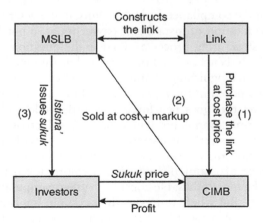

Figure 7.8 Istasna sukuk in operation.

7.3 Sukuk: current position

The Sukuk market is expanding fast; its global size crossed US$715 billion mark in early 2021, with a 3% rise over the year. The Gulf Cooperation Council (GCC) countries are the leaders but Indonesia, Turkey, Malaysia, and Pakistan have emerged as notable contributors. Rapid urbanization in Middle Eastern countries is one of the key factors driving the growth of the market. Furthermore, the diversification of investment patterns in emerging countries and increasing cross-border transactions, are also providing a boost to market growth. Also, various Islamic banking institutions are seeking strategic partnerships with foreign institutions to participate in trade with other countries. In line with this, the governments of these nations are establishing sophisticated Shari'ah-compliant financial institutions with innovative products and services, which are creating a positive outlook for the market.

Furthermore, the widespread adoption of online transaction models has encouraged financial institutions to invest in analytics that can offer better user experience and customized products to their customers. This, along with increasing investments by the governments of Islamic countries for infrastructural development and the digitization of financial services, is projected to drive the market. No wonder it is expected to grow at 18.2% during 2021–2026 on the basis of Bloomberg data.

7.4 Benchmarking

Even though the use of *sukuk* and the volume of funds they have raised have ballooned in recent years, doubts still linger about their *Shari'ah* compliance, especially since 2007, when they nosedived in the wake of Sheikh Taqi Usmani's observation that the bulk of the *sukuk* issued violated the *Shari'ah* norms. The use of *inah* and *tawarruq* in their structuring has raised fresh controversies on the compliance front. In addition, the determination of the markup and the fixation of installment payments have put fresh question marks on their structuring processes. First is the question of the markup rate. It is invariably benchmarked on the London Interbank Offered Rate (Libor). The one distinguishing characteristic of Islamic finance is that its feet are firmly anchored in the *real* economy. In other words, it is productivity-oriented. But the Libor benchmark has little to do with productivity. Interest rate determination is not connected to productivity in any way. It is the result of the central bank's monetary policy and bond placements on the market. Thus, the interest rate benchmarking is not consistent with the basic rationale of Islamic finance. Furthermore, the detachment from the Libor is all the more advisable considering the manipulative fiasco that surrounds it today. But where to turn is the question. Implicit in the search for a benchmark is the recognition that a minimum fixed return component has somehow to be part of an Islamic charge as well. That need must be met without recourse to any rate of interest. One may possibly suggest using 2.5% – the general rate of *zakah* (i.e., the minimum amount a believer with wealth beyond a certain limit is obliged to spend on specified areas, mostly for the benefit of the poor) – as the way to fix flexible markups. There is a sense in his suggestion. Another method could presumably be the construction of a composite index of Islamic banks' gross earnings at centers of Islamic finance. The quarterly moving average of the series at each location may serve as the benchmark for the region and the merger at the global level. Other possibilities could be explored.

Finally, in participatory *sukuk*, such as those based on *mudarabah* or *musharakah*, if a payment installment is to be fixed, the use of the Excel amortization mechanism must be avoided, as it is based on compounding principles. We have demonstrated this in Chapter 5 using the case of home financing. *Sukuk* are the most important financial instruments in the Islamic system, but at the same time, they have given rise to many controversies on the juridical and operational fronts. They lack uniformity in the principles of issuance at the global level and face a variety of challenges in terms of compliance and regulation.

7.5 Summary

- Currently, the policy for operating Islamic finance rests on the presumption that replicating the mainstream products and approach to finance is the only way to attain the range and recognition that is needed to secure a global presence in the industry. The assumption is controversial.
- One of the major consequences of this presumption for ensuring growth has been the appearance of Islamic *sukuk* as a competitor to conventional bonds. *Sukuk* are Islamic bonds, but they are very different from conventional bonds.
- On the demand side for investible funds stand *sukuk* users; they issue *sukuk* as a means to collect resources. On the supply side in the market are the various persons and institutions that want to invest a portion of their incomes as savings; they subscribe to *sukuk* issues on a profit-(loss)-sharing basis.
- Bondholders are not concerned with what happens to the borrower so long as there is no threat to the return of their capital on maturity and the payment of interest thereon is regular. In contrast, *sukuk* holders share profit (loss) with the issuers. As such, they are interested in the success of the projects into which they put their savings. Also, bondholders can always sell their certificates in the secondary market. Such an opportunity is not always available to *sukuk* holders.
- The structuring of *sukuk* for sale is often complex and intricate. Prior and precise decisions have to be made about matters such as the purpose of the *sukuk* issuance; the type of contract(s) that is to be used;

the amount that needs to be raised and approximate maturity time span; the sort of SPV to be created, and so on. Often, one has to use more than one mode in an issue, and the combination has to be smooth and internally consistent. The more complicated a combination is, the greater the chance of noncompliance with *Shari'ah*.

- *Mudarabah* provides a desirable base for *sukuk* issuance because it promotes participatory finance. However, it is not used much because it requires a level of intimacy between the contracting parties, and the increasing social distance of modern times, for a variety of reasons, reduces mutual trust. There is a crisis of mutual trust that gives rise to asymmetric information and leads to risk aversion and aggravating agency problems.
- *Musharakah* is a better basis for floating *sukuk*. Unlike *mudarabah*, here the certificate holders are business *insiders*; they can participate in decision-making processes and supervision of projects where their money is being used if they so choose.
- *Ijara*, or leasing, is usually combined with other modes and is perhaps the leading base for *sukuk* issuance, it being relatively dynamic and more flexible. However, its use in conjunction with buyback provisions has caused much controversy in academic and regulatory circles.

Sukuk based on commodity *murabahah, salam,* and *istisna'* are essentially debt certificates. They often involve the use of *inah* mechanism and have given rise to much difference of opinion within and across countries.

Chapter 8

Risk and risk management

Chapter contents

- Nature of financial risks
- Sources and the types of risks
- Risks: mainstream versus Islamic
- Risk management: meaning and methods
- Risk sharing vs. risk transfer
- Derivatives, futures, and options

Islam bans interest, allowing capital to participate in business ventures only on a profit-and-loss-sharing basis. The possibility of loss is an adversity called risk. Thus, the chapter identifies the main sources of risk and the methods commonly used to reduce or possibly eliminate them. It differentiates between the conventional and Islamic ways of risk treatment and illustrates the use of derivatives, futures, and options in this regard from an Islamic perspective.

8.1 Introduction

Risk refers to the possible occurrence of an adversity in times ahead. It is an *ex ante* entity of a psychic sort. In finance, this adversity is the shrinkage of capital invested in business. The avoidance and mitigation of this adversity are central to risk management. Explorations in the area of financial risks and their management are of recent origin. The theory and practice of risk management are still in the early stages of development. This chapter deals with the identification of financial risks and the methods used to minimize them. The dilemma of risk management is to strike a trade-off between the two opposite forces: the lure for profit and the fear of loss. Figure 8.1

DOI: 10.4324/9781003366973-8

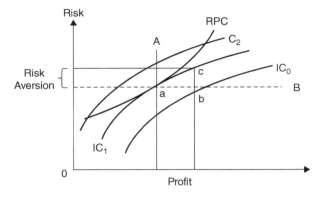

Figure 8.1 Risk aversion.

explains the nature of this trade-off. Here, C_2, C_1, and C_0 are the risk-profit indifference curves of the entrepreneur X, the lower curve showing more or less risk for a given profit along A, while there is more profit for the same risk along B. Other things being equal, X would prefer to be on a lower curve.

RPC is a curve from the map of such *ex ante* curves. In a state of equilibrium an RPC must be tangent to an indifference curve as one is here at point 'a'. Now, if X chooses to stay at 'a', an external observer may call him risk averse. But their difference would be a matter of taste, not of objectivity.

8.2 Risk profit and finance

Explorations in the area of financial risks and their management are of recent origin. The theory and practice of risk management are still in the early stages of their development. To provide you with meaningful insights into the nature and ramifications of the subject, we begin with a brief overview of the capitalist system of risk-taking and its management in a competitive setting.

A primary attribute of competition is its tendency to eliminate economic profit or loss to bring the prices of real goods and services to equality with their costs of production. Economic theorists' search for the source of profit rests in what makes competition imperfect. Frank H. Knight (1921), for example, argued that it was uncertainty born of dynamic change that made competition depart from the ideal profitless state in an economy. Uncertainty breeds risk. Some risks follow probability patterns and can be measured. They can be insured against. In other words, they can be met at a cost.

Thus, for Knight (1921), the remaining certainty that cannot be measured and cannot be insured against by paying a premium, represents the true risk of any business. Uncertainty, so defined, divides society into those who prefer to take risks in the expectation of large gains and those who want to avoid risks in favor of gaining certain, specific, if smaller, incomes. *Risk preference* and *risk aversion* have divided human societies, regardless of time and space, into the broad categories of hired and unhired factors of production. Entrepreneurs fall into the unhired category. They guarantee specific, fixed returns to the hired factors of production – lenders, workers, and property owners – in the form of interest, wages, and rent. Entrepreneurs choose to be claimants of the residual business earnings in the expectations of large gains but simultaneously have to expose their investment to the risk of shrinkage (loss) if revenue receipts belie expectations and fall short of payments made to the hired factors.

Islamic banks operate in a capitalist system in competition with their conventional counterparts. They cannot do business in defiance of the systemic requirements. They can observe the Islamic ban on interest but would find it difficult to survive without credit creation and the risks associated with it. Even though most participants involved in economic processes are exposed to some sort of risk, here we are concerned only with the risks relating to financing activities in modern economies – i.e., the loss of capital. Macroeconomics theory teaches us that real goods and services in an economy have circular flows which are matched by the reverse money flows of national products that can be accounted for as national output, income, or expenditure. Capitalism not only presupposes the existence of hired factors of production – workers, land, credit, and the natural resources sharing these flows; it also presupposes the existence of an *initial* facility of finance provided by bank credit that enables entrepreneurs to pay for wages and hold inventory.

A recent unconventional view gaining currency is that finance is a sort of invisible *ex ante* flow extending resource availability into the future. The view seems to hold some element of truth; it links well with Keynes's (1957) recognition of money as a financial asset. This recognition led to viewing money as an interest-bearing claim the banks could create or destroy at will in response to variations in demand.

8.3 Islam and financial risks

A distinctive feature of the more recent discussions on Islamic banking has been the growing wedge between its classical theory and current practice. The evolution of theoretical positions on Islamic banking owes much to the early writers on the subject. Those positions continue to find occasional expression and support even in more recent literature on the subject. Nevertheless, the structural design of the instruments and practices of Islamic banking are, of late, being distanced from these initial positions by the newer generations of Islamic scholars, especially in Malaysia. As a result, while the theoretical edifice of Islamic banking remains rooted in the classical presumption that participatory *risk-sharing* modes – *mudarabah* and *musharakah* – are, or should be the *only* fulcrum of Islamic finance, its practice is fast moving away from that theory. The fixed return financing modes are tending to gain dominance worldwide.

Despite the concerted efforts of central bank authorities, to date, the overall proportion of risk-sharing contracts in Islamic finance could barely cross the 20% mark across the globe. Writers on the subject are aware of the causes of this dominance and do not lack suggestions to remedy the situation, but here is not the place to discuss these issues in any detail. Suffice it to say, the theory-practice divide in Islamic banking seems to be hindering the diversification of instruments that are required for the rapid growth of Islamic banking

A distinctive feature of the more recent discussions on Islamic banking has been the growing wedge between its classical theory and current practice. The evolution of theoretical positions on Islamic banking owes much to the early writers on the subject. Those positions continue to find occasional expression and support even in more recent literature on the subject. Nevertheless, the structural design of the instruments and practices of Islamic banking is, of late, being distanced from these initial positions by the newer generations of Islamic scholars, especially in Malaysia. As a result, while the theoretical edifice of Islamic banking remains rooted in the classical presumption that participatory *risk-sharing* modes – *mudarabah* and *musharakah* – are or should be the *only* fulcrum of Islamic finance, its practice is fast moving away from that theory. The fixed return financing modes are tending to gain dominance worldwide.

Despite the concerted efforts of central bank authorities, to date, the overall proportion of risk-sharing contracts in Islamic finance could barely cross the 20% mark across the globe. Writers on the subject are aware of the causes of this dominance and do not lack suggestions to remedy the situation, but here is not the place to discuss these issues in any detail. Suffice it to say, the theory-practice divide in Islamic banking seems to be hindering the diversification of instruments that are required for the rapid growth of Islamic banking.

While there were many – perhaps more powerful – reasons for the prohibition of interest in Islam, the early writers highlighted one in particular: interest is not allowable because it confers a gain on the capital owners without them bearing any of the business risks. They seized upon this apparent difference between the interest that Islam banned and the profit from trade that it allowed. "No risk, no gain" was indeed paraded as an inviolable precept in the area of banking and finance. This implied that it was a predetermination of interest without regard to the outcome of business that kept it free of risk and thus constituted the primary reason for its prohibition. Surprisingly, most of the scholarly writings and doctoral dissertations in the area of Islamic banking continue to stick to the "no risk, no gain" precept as an article of faith. Of course, its validity in the case of profit from business cannot be disputed. Disputed is the validity of the wrap such writings attempt to put around the precept. For what is being said is that no gain can be legitimate in Islam unless there is a counter-risk to bear. The stand shows not only ignorance of the realities on the ground but also shows little realization that the exclusion of these realities conflicts with some rules that do grant fixed returns to investors. Most deferred payment contracts, for instance, fall in this category, and jurists authenticate them as allowable.

Arguably, the "no risk, no gain" rule promotes a venturesome attitude toward business but does not grant a license for reckless risk-taking. In mitigation, Islam prohibits inequity, *gharar*, speculation, and gambling from affecting business. The distinction Knight made between insurable and uninsurable risks lost significance over time, as it was based on complicated probability calculations and reduced profit to windfall gains resulting from errors of forecasting.

Furthermore, in real life, firms usually choose to internalize many risks that could in fact be insured against and met at a cost. Risk is an *ex ante* concept. It is conditioned by an individual's state of mind; it defies cardinal measurement. Meaningful concepts of profit are also *ex ante* and inaccurate. *Ex post* profit, therefore, cannot be put in a one-on-one relationship with risk. Possibly, this is why Islam does not seek such a relationship; it puts no ceiling on business profits. Once the presence of risk is established, *Shari'ah* sets no limit on profit provided no Islamic norms are violated to earn it. Islamic ethics seeks to hedge human conduct so that businesses' earnings look reasonable. However, Ghazali laments that Islamic norms tend to restrict profit so that they remain legitimate, but unfortunately, people are invariably not satisfied with small gains and are prone to violate the norms. Conventional economic theories talk of normal, moderate, or abnormal profit. Such distinctions have little relevance from an Islamic point of view.

Even though risks defy cardinal measurement, risks can be ranked as high or low. Ranking suggests possibilities of dealing with risks. Risks can be diff used, reduced or can perhaps be eliminated in some cases. Diffusion is a process of spreading the risk quantum over as wide a range as possible. Combining the sale of as many items as possible under one roof in a supermarket tends to diffuse financial risk for the owners. Diffusion is a major tool for insurance companies. The division of corporate equity capital in shares of smaller denominations serves the same end. Diffusion tends to reduce risk. The institutions of limited liability, or the pursuit of cheap money policy and the granting of protection or subsidies, all intend to work in the same direction. The enlargement of corporate size through mergers and acquisitions also helps to reduce risk. The Islamic abolition of interest and the sharing of returns promote risk diffusion and help to reduce their

96 Risk and risk management

rigor. Dealing with various types of risk is an integral part of corporate management.

8.3.1 Risk management

Literature on risk and risk management has proliferated in recent years and broadly covers macroeconomic policies, technological design, and financing. Even though we are concerned here only with financial risk, you must always keep in mind the hired and unhired factors of production. Elaborate on the economic consequences of this division and the consequences for the firm of getting things wrong can indeed prove serious, inflicting a loss of opportunity, a loss of business, and a loss of goodwill. Thus, risk management is a complicated affair and may by itself prove a more risky business than what it seeks to ward off. Risk management requires the acumen and self-restraint of an artist.

8.3.2 The requirements

Financial risks, in essence, refer to the possibilities of corporate net assets falling short of meeting their current liabilities and obligations. Such possibilities arise because of the uncertainties that characterize financial markets; vagaries make the course of events and their impact unpredictable. Suppliers and users of funds both face financial risks that have varied sources. Risk management helps a company identify specific exposures, especially those that could result in losing wealth measured in money. Protection of wealth constitutes one of the major *Shari'ah* objectives and implies support for risk management. As a general rule, firms have a better chance of survival by adapting to risks rather than attempting to eliminate them completely. Sound risk management broadly requires (i) the regular assessment of risks, (ii) action to pre-empt or reduce them, or (iii) action to tolerate them, if possible. The possibility of failing to eliminate or reduce a risk, or of it crossing the tolerance limit, cannot be ignored. Thus, it is always advisable to have a contingency plan ready at hand. Sound risk management is essential for setting up a business and making it succeed.

It aims at generating ideas and promoting good managerial practices in general. It requires the sharing of information and expertise with others. This can help the business identify the areas where it could lose money. Improving the flow of information tends to prevent management from unconsciously looking inwards and therefore issuing out on potential areas of expansion. A helicopter view of the whole enterprise gives a better sense of what might cause failure regardless of specific risk exposures, such as the bankruptcy of a borrower. Financial exposures include various types of risk, ranging from simple bank credit to foreign exchange transactions. Let us have a look at the main risk sources from an Islamic perspective and see how they are managed.

8.3.3 Types of risk

Businesses face innumerable risks, all of which are difficult to list and explain. Economists, therefore, classify them into broad categories for analytical purposes on the basis of some common characteristics. The main types of risk are briefly discussed as follows.

8.3.3.1 Market risk

Market risk refers to the expectation of loss arising from factors that affect the *overall* performance of the financial markets. The shrinkage of the market because of the current financial crisis (2007–2008) and the collapse of banks across the world is an illustration of market-initiated risks. Other sources of market risk in more recent years include political turmoil, such as that in Syria or Egypt; external aggression, such as the US-led invasion of Iraq or Afghanistan; interest rate manipulations, such as the manipulation of the LIBOR by leading banks; natural calamities, such as the Japanese tsunami; or the 2008 terrorist attacks in Mumbai. These market risks are of a blanket sort. They are mostly rooted in the system and hence are called 'systemic'. Diversification cannot eliminate such risks, even macroeconomic policies are needed.

However, investors may have specific or nonsystemic risks in the market as well. The source of such risks could, for example, include unfavorable movements in the prices of goods, say raw cotton, that serve as inputs for a firm's production in a specific industry – cotton textiles. The risk here is tied directly to the performance of a particular security – e.g., shares of cotton textile companies. Another example could be of a company whose stock you own going bankrupt, thus making your investment worthless. We can guard against such risks in some measure through investment diversification. As there has to be an inseparable linkage between financial transactions and real assets in Islamic finance, market risks assume added importance in the system. The Islamic Financial Services Board (IFSB) defines market risk as the possibility of losses in-and-off balance sheet positions arising from movements in market prices. Balance sheet positions refer to those that could arise due to both the recording and nonrecording of some transactions in the accounts of the firm. This suggests that the focus of attention in Islamic finance essentially has to be on dealing with nonsystemic market risks.

This is clear from the practice of Islamic banks benchmarking the price of various financial instruments on some rate, mostly the London interbank offered rate of interest – the LIBOR. The linkage of financial transactions with real economic activity in the Islamic system creates two additional risks for the banks. One is the possible mark-up variation in *murabahah* due to fluctuations in the benchmark LIBOR. This can possibly be avoided if Islamic banks shift to using, for example, the *zakah* rate standardized at

2.5% as the benchmark. The second risk stems from the possible fall in the prices of real assets, such as the assets underlying financial transactions that the banks have to keep holding for some time

8.3.3.2 Credit risk

Credit risk causes a business to lose money if a partner, or a customer, is unable to pay the amount owed or defaults on installments, say, home financing. This may happen if the partner or the client files for bankruptcy or is facing a temporary cash crunch. Closure of contracts that depend on counter-party performance is quite risky. Such situations may, for example, arise in *salam* or *istisna'*. Both are preproduction contracts where payment is made before the goods are to be delivered. The risk is that the delivery may not take place or may be delayed or the goods do not meet the agreed quality. Similarly, there is risk in *mudarabah* contracts too, where the entrepreneur may not pay the profit share to the financier at all or when it is due. Such credit risks may arise, despite the parties being honest, due to systemic reasons or due to contract-specific factors, such as nonsymmetric information or unforeseeable problems arising because of technological or natural factors. One way to reduce credit risks seems to be minimizing a firm's dependence on credit.

8.3.3.3 Fiduciary risk

Fiduciary risk normally arises in principal-agent contractual relationships. The risk arises when the agent is not operating in the best interest of the principal. One measure of such performance is the optimization of the principal's gain out of given resources. Not doing so means that the agent has failed to discharge his fiduciary (legal) responsibility in full. A fund manager may, for example, over-multiply transactions for a client, risking the erosion of earnings due to rising transaction costs. However, the failure does not necessarily involve foul play. Agency relationships are probably more common and crucial in Islamic finance. For example, Islamic banks treat demand deposits as *qard hasan* (benevolent loans) and offer no return on them, just as the current deposits are treated in mainstream banks. In either case, there is nothing that debars banks from using the money in the way they want. It follows that demand deposits deserve greater protection than investment deposits. Also, care has to be taken that any risk that the investment deposits face is not transferred or transmitted to the demand deposit holders.

8.3.3.4 Shari'ah noncompliance risk

Financial products and services in the Islamic system are mostly replicas of their conventional counterparts; the two look quite similar, especially in terms of their economic consequences. The distinction between them is created because Islamic products are invariably structured in such a way that they comply and stay compliant with the juridical principles and standards in letter and spirit. Thus, *Shari'ah* noncompliance risk refers to the possibility of an Islamic financial service or product being found to be not in line with established *Shari'ah* principles and standards. For instance, we have shown earlier how home financing contracts resemble the conventional arrangement if they use the Excel formula for the purpose of amortization. Three sources of risk-bearing noncompliance may be identified: The first is the uncalled-for desire to compete with conventional banks, which can lead to an indiscrete imitation of their ways in *every* sphere of financing. Note that the share of the formal Islamic system in total financial assets worldwide is no more than 1/180 at present (2012); the competition between the two is akin to that between a candle and the sun. Second, the final say of secular civil courts in financial disputes tends to create problems for Islamic financial institutions, even in Muslim countries.

Harmonization, which has now been ensured in Malaysia, is welcome.

Finally, there is a great scarcity of *Shari'ah* scholars who are well versed not only in Islamic law but also in mainstream economic and financial disciplines to sit on the advisory boards of Islamic institutions. The fiasco around *Shari'ah* compliance of *sukuk* in 2008 has been a lesson-giving experience. Periodic summer schools with refresher courses in these areas may prove helpful.

8.3.3.5 Liquidity risk

Liquidity in economics refers to the ease and speed with which one asset can be converted into another. On those criteria, a car is less liquid an asset than gold, or treasury bills are more liquid than corporate bonds. Evidently, money (cash) is the most liquid form of wealth. It can readily be converted into other assets without inquiry. Banks essentially deal in costs or liquidity. As banks operate on a fractional reserve principle, there is a trade-off between profit (from lending or investment) and liquidity in their business. Subject to this trade-off being judicious, maintaining as much liquidity in their assets as possible is the guiding principle of banking. Note that in the structure of a bank balance sheet, the assets are arranged in descending order based on their relative liquidity – cash appearing at the top, buildings at the bottom. Compare it with the assets listing in a business corporation.

Liquidity risk is the possibility of a reduction in current or future earnings or capital stock arising from the inability of a bank to meet its obligations on time. It includes the failure to manage an unplanned decrease in funding sources. Liquidity risk also underlines the inability of a bank to recognize or deal with changes in market conditions that hinder the quick liquidation of assets with minimal loss. Paraphrasing the IFSB, one may define liquidity risk for the Islamic financial instruments (IFIs) as the

100 Risk and risk management

Figure 8.2 The risk wheel.

potential loss arising from their inability to meet obligations or to fund increases in payables, as they fall due without increasing unacceptable costs. And there are reasons that make Islamic financial institutions more open to liquidity risks than conventional banking institutions. These include the predominance of and damage to their reputations. Figure 8.1 debt-based orientation of the IFIs assets, the lack of short-term compliant securities in the financial markets, and the lack of appropriate legal infrastructures. These factors may make IFIs more open to instability. Figure 8.2 summarizes the risks to which the IFIs are exposed short-term compliant securities in the financial markets and the lack of financial instruments (IFIs) as the potential loss arising from their inability to meet obligations or to fund increases in payables, as they fall due without increasing unacceptable costs.

8.3.3.6 Foreign exchange risk

Foreign exchange risk refers to the possibility of businesses facing a loss due to adverse variations in exchange rates. This is also known as currency risk. Exporters and importers usually face currency risk, but individuals making investments abroad or employed there are not immune to exposure. For example, if the ringgit-dollar rate is lower when the investment is redeemed than when it was made, the investor is liable to lose money. Consider the following example explaining currency risk. Suppose an Indian firm sells ready-made garments to a supermarket in the United States for US$1 million, with the domestic price of the dollar at the time of the contract being INR55. Payment is received after three months. During the interval, the rupee appreciated to 54.5 to the dollar. Thus, exchange rate variation makes the firms suffer a loss of (55–54.5) 1,000,000 = INR 500,000. Individual investors investing their savings in a foreign country may face identical problems. Islam treats foreign currencies as a different sort of money and thus allows trading in them.

8.3.3.7 Other risks

Figure 8.2 lists a few more risks in addition to those we have already discussed. These include, for example, risks relating to equity investment, rate of return, and a firm's operations. However, such risks are common to all financing activities; there is little in them that can be labeled as special to Islamic finance. In brief, equity investment always carries the risk of shrinkage in value due to unforeseen factors, especially due to speculation or financial turmoil. Likewise, the rate of return risk refers to the chance of return on investment becoming negative. We have postponed the discussion of an important type – the displaced commercial risk – to a later chapter.

8.4 Enterprise risk management framework

Business risks are on the rise in an increasingly unpredictable world. Investors and employees seek greater security. The magnitude, variety, and range of risks continue to grow unabated. Under the circumstances, risk management has become a major concern in modern business. As mentioned earlier, risks can be ranked as high or low, but their cardinal measurement is mostly impossible. What we identify as risk measurement tools are in fact ways to minimize risk, as the complete elimination of a business risk is rarely possible. The variety of risks is so large that a common strategy to minimize or eliminate them is difficult to conceive. However, a broad general framework known as Enterprise Risk Management (ERM) is often suggested. It consists of methods and processes that organizations can use to manage risks. It helps them to seize the opportunities conducive to achieving their objectives.

The ERM framework involves identifying particular events or circumstances related to the risks and opportunities relevant to achieving organizational goals. It guides firms to evaluate a risk, the chance of its occurrence, and its likely impact. It helps them in determining a response to problems and monitoring the progress made. The ERM thus makes a firm proactive in addressing risks; it enables business enterprises to protect and create value for their stakeholders, including owners, employees, and customers.

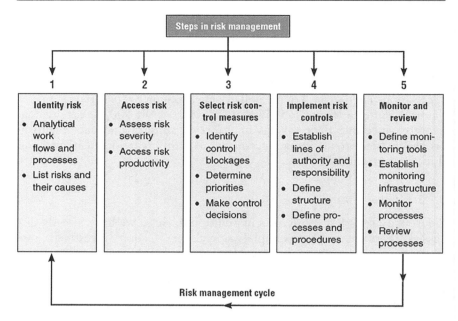

Figure 8.3 Risk management cycle.
Source: Adapted from MetricStream, http://www.metricstream.com/solution_briefs/ORM.htm

ERM promotes overall societal well-being. It provides a risk-based approach to managing any enterprise and is quite popular with manufacturing and engineering firms.

However, ERM entered the arsenal of business firms rather late. Here, it integrates concepts of internal control, including audit and accounting, *Shari'ah* compliance, human resource development, capital adequacy norms, ratings, and so on, in an overall strategic plan. ERM attends to the needs of various stakeholders, who want to understand the broad spectrum of risks confronting complex organizations to aid their appropriate and gainful management. Regulators and debt-rating agencies have increased their vigil on the risk management frameworks of financial enterprises. Figure 8.3 provides an overview of the risk management process. It shows the sequence of the main steps involved and a circular relationship, making ERM a significant, integrated and cohesive tool. The actions to be taken under each step are also outlined.

8.4.1 Derivatives and risk mitigation

In the most general terms, financial risk refers to the extent of adverse change in the price of a security relative to a given change in some connected variable. Businesses attempt to hedge these risks and mostly use derivatives for that purpose. Derivatives work as financial instruments that are based on initial instruments having the same or similar characteristics as the assets and liabilities that specify the company's risk position as per the balance sheet or have no intrinsic value. Like the moon, a derivative has no asset underlying it. Derivatives don't have a light of their own; they only reflect the light of the sun – i.e., the value of the asset underlying them. Derivatives have no intrinsic value.

Derivatives inherently tend to carry more risk than the instruments on which they are based; they combine the risks associated with the underlying asset with their own. Thus, derivatives should be used only if part of the risk to be tackled remains after the management has exhausted all conceivable policy alternatives. For example, hedging financial risks is not free of cost: you have to pay for the brokerage and deposit 5% of the price at the time of the contract and the remaining amount on maturity. Financial risks multiply at a fast pace in range and magnitude; their dynamism tends to associate low probabilities with high gains. Media amplifications and public policies tend to distort risk perceptions, making their assessment quite difficult.

As Islamic finance utilizes virtually the same mechanisms that are used in conventional finance, one must note that the main difference in their derivative applications is in the case of debt instruments. The nature of debt instruments in conventional finance is such that *Shari'ah* does not accept them; the direct linkage with real assets is missing. Thus, these instruments cannot be the basis of tradable securities. Thus, many problems concerning derivatives in Islamic finance remain unresolved. We cannot go into the details of the debate in this introductory reading. Suffice it to say, presently, derivatives are controversial in Islamic finance literature. The AAOIFI clearly disallows derivative instruments in the form of futures, options, and swaps, although it approves their qualified use in organized commodity markets (Standard 20: 359–371). The ground reality is that the industry has shown little aversion to using derivatives. Here, we discuss the nature of those derivative instruments that Islam is perceived as allowing and the areas of their application that Islam permits.

The areas identified for using derivatives are essentially hedging risks relating to foreign exchange and profit rates. However, it must be pointed out here that CDs are available for pairing with only four major world currencies: the US dollar, the European euro, the Japanese yen, and the UK pound – the US dollar leads the pack. A derivative contract cannot be sold or purchased except for a specified minimum amount. Note also that trading in derivatives does not exist in most developing economies, including Malaysia.

8.4.2 Exchange risk hedging

Businesses and investors face foreign exchange risk on account of possible adverse changes in the currency rates during a contract period. To avoid this risk, they do not even welcome the possibility of benefiting from the

104 Risk and risk management

likelihood of a favorable change. Thus, firms aim to avoid *all* changes in the exchange rate, both favorable and unfavorable. They are interested only in their trading gains. Derivative instruments help them to reduce such risks.

Let us go back to our currency risk example. The Indian firm suffers a loss of 500,000 rupees due to an adverse movement in the domestic price of the US dollar. How could derivative use have eliminated or reduced this risk of loss? The firm in our illustration can sell a foreign exchange (FX) future on the Indian National Stock Exchange for US$1,000,000 on the date of signing the contract, say 30 September 2012, at the current rate of INR 54.45 to a dollar to be delivered three months later, in December 2012. Suppose on that date the spot quotation for the dollar is INR 54.15. The position of the firm would be as shown next.

Exporter: The firm that exported ready-made garments worth US$1,000,000 in September 2012 wants protection against possible appreciation of the Indian rupee in December 2012 – i.e., wzhen it has to receive the payment from the supermarket. The firm wants to lock in the exchange rate for the transaction. It will operate as follows:

One INR – US$ contract size	US$1,000
Sell 1,000 INR – US$ December 2012 contracts (on 30 September 2012)	INR54.4500 per dollar
Buy 1,000 INR – US$ December 2012 contracts in December 2012	INR54.1500 per dollar

Sell US$1,000,000 in Spot market at 54.15 in December 2012 (assuming that the Indian rupee depreciated initially but later appreciated to 54.15 per US$ by the end of December 2012, as foreseen by the firm)

Profit/loss from futures (December 2012)	1,000 * 1,000 *(54.45–54.15) = 0.30 *1,000 * 1,000 = INR300,000

The net receipt in INR for the hedged transaction would be 1,000,000 *54.15 + 300,000 = 54,150,000 + 300,000 = INR54,450,000. Had the firm not participated in the futures market, the firm would have only received INR54,150,000. However, it kept its sales unexposed to Forex rate risk.

Now let us consider the case of an Indian firm that imports on 30 September 2012 computers from the United States worth US$1,000,000, the INR/US$ rate being 54.45. Payment is due after three months. Here, the risk of the firm does not consist of a fall in the exchange rate but in its rise. To eliminate or reduce this risk the importer can purchase a forward contract. The process would work out as follows

---

Importer: The firm importing computers worth US$1,000,000 in September 2012 wants protection against a possible depreciation of the Indian rupee in December 2012 – i.e., when it has to make the payment to the manufacturers in the United States. The firm wants to lock in the exchange rate for the transaction. It will operate as follows:

One INR – US$ contract size	US$1,000
Purchase 1,000 INR – US$ December 2012 contracts (on 30 September 2012)	INR54.6500 per dollar
Sell 1,000 INR – US$ December 2012 contracts in December 2012	INR54.4500 per dollar

Buy US$1,000,000 in Spot market at 54.65 in December 2012 (assuming that the Indian rupee appreciated initially but later depreciated to 54.65 per US$ by the end of December 2012, as foreseen by the firm)

Profit/loss from futures (December 2012)

$$1,000 * 1,000 * (54.45\text{--}54.65)$$
$$= -0.20 * 1,000 * 1,000$$
$$= \text{INR} -200,000$$

The net receipt in INR for the hedged transaction would be 1,000,000 * 54.65 – 200,000 = 54,650,000 – 200,000 = INR54,450,000. Had the firm not participated in the futures market, the firm would have to pay only INR54,450,000, not INR54,650.000. Thus, the importer kept his purchases unexposed to Forex rate risk.

8.4.3 Options

Options are variants of derivatives that grant the holder a right to sell or purchase the underlying asset for a price without any counter obligation. For instance, you may reserve a house from a builder for RM300,000 with the option to buy or not within three months. The builder agrees to wait for your decision for a charge of 0.5% of the agreed price – i.e., RM1500 for waiting. If after three months you decide not to buy the house for whatever reason, you lose RM1500, the amount for which the builder had sold you the option. If a right is purchased, as here, the contract is called a call option. Likewise, a trader who believes that the price of a particular stock will rise might buy a call option to purchase the stock at a fixed price instead of purchasing the stock. If the stock price at expiration is above the contracted price and thus yields a net gain, he will purchase the stock; alternatively, he will let the call contract expire without action, losing only the premium amount. A trader who believes that a stock price will increase can buy the stock or sell a put. The trader selling a put has an obligation to buy the stock from the put buyer at the put buyer's option.

8.4.4 Swaps

A financial swap is a derivative contract where one party agrees to exchange or "swap" the cash inflows from one asset for another. Companies use swaps to avoid variations over time in the cash inflows from an asset. For example, a company paying a variable rate of interest may swap its interest payments with another to pay the first company a fixed periodic rate. The underlying asset gives the swap its name. Thus, the asset could, for example, be the rate of interest, a commodity, credit default, or total return. However,

106 Risk and risk management

Table 8.1 Swap operation illustration

Period	1	2	3	4	5	6	
Company A (%)	6.4	3.1	4.2	3.5	2.3	6.6	%
Company B (%)	4.35	4.35	4.35	4.35	4.35	4.35	%

some sorts of swaps are on the way out. Intercontinental Exchange, the authority responsible for LIBOR, will stop publishing one-week and two-month LIBOR after December 31, 2021. A simple hypothetical explanatory illustration follows. Table 8.1 gives the interest rates that Company A is to receive from borrowers on varying amounts over the next three years. To avoid fluctuations, it swaps its receivables for an agreed price with Company B to provide a uniform average semi-annual return of 4.35%

8.5 IFSB guidelines

Operating under juristic constraints, IFIs face distinctive risks, and their methods of managing them are also in some measure different from the conventional system. To keep them on course, in 2005, the IFSB published comprehensive guidelines for IFIs (excluding insurance) to manage risks. These include the following:

- The IFIs must have in place a comprehensive risk management and reporting system with appropriate board senior executives to identify, measure, monitor, report, and control allowable risks, including norms for capital adequacy.
- They must install an appropriate risk management system, and the directors of the bank must deal with the overall objectives, strategies, and specific methods employed for risk management.
- An appropriate risk measurement system must be set up in each institution. The system may use standards and issue reports, impose limits, and establish rules and investment guidelines. Incentives and compensations may also be employed. Adequate internal controls may be put into operation.
- Finally, there are guidelines for managing specific risks, including the ones we have listed earlier. The thrust of these guidelines is that caution and compliance with *Shari'ah* norms are to be the guideposts in risk management while using the conventional tools we have discussed.

Markets for derivatives doubtless play a crucial role in the reduction of risks, but of late, the lure of rising leverage gains has converted them into unregulated dens of high-risk credit bets; they can cook up any kind of leverage device, including caps, collars, and floors, to bet whatever they like out of virtually anything. Some 25 years ago, the derivatives market was small and domestic. Since then it has grown, impressively – around 24% per year in the last decade – into a sizable global market.

8.6 Summary

- Perfect competition does not allow economic profit. Dynamic change in society makes competition.
- Imperfect and gives rise to uncertainty. Uncertainty breeds risk and divides society into risk takers (entrepreneurs), who accept great risk in the hope of larger gains, and risk averters –the hired factors who prefer more secure incomes even if those incomes are smaller. Entrepreneurs are capital owners or have command over productive resources. They guarantee fixed incomes to the hired factors and become residual claimers to the revenues generated – the profit (loss). Thus, capitalism becomes a profit-and-loss system.
- The logic of capitalism presupposes the existence of not only the hirable factors of production – the workers and the owners of natural resources – but also an initial availability of bank credit to pay for wages and to hold inventory. There is or ought to be a well-oiled financial system. Since profit is uncertain, and there is even a risk of losing capital, risk management is imperative for the growth of firms, industries, and the economy.
- Since the Islamic economic system has a close affinity with certain basic elements of capitalism, Islamic finance has adopted many capitalist practices but not those to do with interest, indeterminacy or ambiguity (*gharar*), and speculation. Thus, the subject of risk management has emerged in Islamic writings. However, the practice of Islamic finance differs considerably from its theoretical positions.
- While theory adheres to the classical legacy of the "no risk, no gain" precept as the guiding star of the system, in practical terms, most actual financing remains debt-based.
- Risk diffusion and diversification have been among the important methods of managing risks over the centuries and involve little cost compared with modern techniques.
- Seeking, enriching, and sharing knowledge, information, and experience about risks and their nature can make the task of risk management easier and more cost-effective.
- There are various types of financial risk, including price risk, credit risk, *Shari'ah*-compliant risks, liquidity risk, foreign exchange risk, and so on. It is difficult to exhaust the list as new sources of risks continue to pop up as new sorts of businesses come into existence with the passage of time.
- Various derivatives emerged as hedging tools for risk management and swamped the financial markets in a short time. Their presence remains

108 Risk and risk management

unabated. However, hedging comes with a cost. The cost can be viewed as a premium paid for insuring against specific risks.

- Derivatives assume various forms: forwards, futures, options – call and put options – and swaps, etc. Trading in derivatives is itself quite risky and requires skill, self-restraint, patience, and probably a bit of luck as well.
- Although there are reservations about the use of derivatives in Islamic finance, they continue to exist. Powerful *Shari'ah* bodies and regulators have allowed their use subject to some stringent conditions and supervisory controls. The derivatives that Islamic banks use or can use reflect many features of conventional finance tools but are still differentiated products.

Chapter 9

Islam and insurance (takaful)

Chapter contents

- Insurance: concept and evolution
- Basic principles, insurable interest
- Islam and insurance
- Indemnity, underwriting
- Takaful modes and models
- Re-takaful

In a way, this chapter continues the discussion of the preceding one, as insurance is an important way of hedging against risks that are nonfinancial in character but involve finance. The institutions that handle the financing are not the customary banks but insurance companies. *Takaful* is the Islamic counterpart of conventional insurance, but it differs from the former because it has to meet some juristic requirements. The issue of a life insurance cover in *takaful* remains controversial, although it can be acquired under the umbrella of "family *takaful*". There are other limitations too. This chapter provides a brief account of the evolution of mainstream insurance concepts and practices and elaborates why and how *takaful* departs from conventional insurance in matters of outlook approach and applications.

9.1 Introduction

Future breeds uncertainty and carries events for individuals, groups, and societies with consequences – good or bad – unknown until they unfold. The favorable ones are welcome, but the adverse ones like illness, fire, floods, and wars may threaten our health, property, and even existence. Unable to block such adverse happenings, people seek ways to get some

DOI: 10.4324/9781003366973-9

compensation, however poor, in money terms. The trillion-dollar insurance business is the result of this search. Muslims have not been slow in having an Islamic version. The industry runs on probability distributions and the law of averages. The instrument is a contract, contained in what is known as a 'policy', in which an individual or a business, usually a company, undertakes, to compensate the policyholder for the damage insured against as per the contract terms and procedure, the consideration being the periodic payments called the 'premium'.

9.1.1 Insurance concept

The outcome of the business decisions individuals or institutions take in the face of uncertainty about the future course of events may turn out to be favorable to them or unfavorable. Favorable outcomes are welcome, but the possibility of unfavorable ones occurring is worrisome as the damage caused can be beyond repair. Limiting the risk of possible loss of investment or its transfer to somewhere else is invariably a preferred outcome in business. The first step in that direction was the introduction of the principle of keeping the liability of stockholders in modern corporations limited to the value of their subscriptions. This encouraged people to invest in business ventures.

The second was the provision of a compensatory business from the beginning until the end. When the job is done, the accounts are prepared to analyze whether the business has made any profit. Only when the profit is realized can it be shared between the participants and the operator. This means that the operator will have to be very cautious in using the money paid by the participants. On the other hand, the *wakalah* model allows the operator to take the commission upfront. Whether the business is profitable or not, the operator has already obtained their commission. As a business enterprise, the operator prefers the *wakalah* to the mudarabah model. All other aspects of the business are quite similar to the mainstream, which constitute the pillars of modern capitalism raised on the foundation of interest.

9.1.2 Evolution: Brief history

The concept of insurance has existed since the very dawn of human civilization, although it has not always been known as 'insurance'. The history of its evolution is quite fascinating. Human beings have been familiar with risk – to their life and possessions – since Adam first set foot on Earth. The concept of risk minimization and cooperation for mutual benefit is rooted in our basic human instinct of fellow feeling. For example, if a person lost his house in a fire, his neighbors would help him to rebuild it. However, the first arrangements that come close to our modern conception of insurance probably emerged along the trade routes of ancient China and Babylon.

During the BC era, traders used to distribute their merchandise over a number of ships to limit their loss if any single ship sank negotiating river rapids or on a long sea voyage. It is on record that early Mediterranean traders used a well-established practice to hedge against financial risk: whenever a trader borrowed funds to purchase a cargo with which he could trade, he would pay the lender an amount in addition to what he borrowed provided the lender would promise to cancel the loan in case the shipment was stolen or lost on the high seas. The additional amount promised was in the nature of a premium for insurance coverage. In the case of a mishap taking place, the lender will lose this money. The shipowners would also come together to devise ways of minimizing risk and to help each other in the case of goods being lost due to piracy, accident, or disaster.

However, over time, technologies improved and multiplied fast, production processes became increasingly diverse and complicated, and economic systems became more complex. With these and other developments, businesses required more and more funding. Larger sums needed to be invested and, as a result, the risks also grew. It soon became clear that friends helping friends and business owners coming to the rescue of fellow business owners in their hour of need were no longer sufficient to ward off the various sorts of risks. Organized effort was required. Insurance had to be institutionalized.

The process of formalizing insurance probably started with the decision of British merchants to underwrite cargoes that had to make perilous voyages overseas in search of new profit opportunities. Insurance (underwriting) was smart business to protect investments in lucrative businesses. But the underwriters were essentially financiers. They needed agents to market the concept and to promote their business. This led to the foundation of insurance companies. The first insurance company was formed in 1667, a year after the great fire of London destroyed over 13,000 houses and businesses.

The company was named *The Fire Office*, and its purpose was to insure homes. Insurance emerged in the USA rather late, but for the same purpose: the Philadelphia Contributionship for the Insurance of Houses from Loss by Fire was established in 1752 by Benjamin Franklin. However, the American company declared that houses made of wood were uninsurable.

The risks of losing merchandise on the high seas and of fire destroying property were simple to perceive, but both represented a specialized sort of cover for the types of risk faced by business owners. Soon the need for insurance coverage began to spread to more diverse areas. Individuals and businesses today own an array of assets exposed to various types of risk and need protection. Insurance is now broadly divided into life assurance and general insurance categories, offering contracts, called policies, for any insurable interest. To illustrate, insurance policies cover asset theft, accident, health, flood and earthquake damage, etc. Insurance companies such as Lloyds of London, established in 1688, and AIG in the USA are among the international giants. Insurance business today holds and manages large global funds and assets.

9.2 Basic principles

9.2.1 Good faith

Insurance business, including *takaful*, operates on the basis of "utmost good faith" because there is an intrinsic imbalance in the information to which the parties have access. It is therefore essential that the parties to an insurance contract make a full declaration of all material facts in the insurance agreement. The insurer and the insured must observe a minimum standard of honesty in their statements and behavior toward each other; one is not supposed to mislead or withhold critical information from the other. Each party is duty bound to voluntarily disclose accurate and full material pertaining to the risk covered whether the other party requests it or not. Failure to do so nullifies the contract.

9.2.2 Insurable interest

Initially, the business of insurance tended to resemble gambling because there were no firm criteria for deciding what sort of risks one could or could not seek to cover. It was in the last quarter of the eighteenth century in the United Kingdom that the presence of an *insurable interest* became a prerequisite for acquiring the cover. An insurable interest can be established either on the basis of factual expectation in a particular case or on the basis of legal reasoning. We expect, and *in fact* experience, a person as having a natural interest in the continued life of his wife and children; he might suffer great emotional loss from their demise. He thus has an insurable interest in their lives. The risk of destruction or damage to an asset, say a person's house or car, confronts the owner with a financial loss. The owner has a legal right to protect his/her property from fire or theft. Here, the law creates an insurable interest for the owner to seek cover against financial loss, both in Islamic and in conventional finance.

In the Islamic system, family *takaful* is based on factual expectations in preference to individual life insurance. It relates to one of the leading *Shari'ah* objectives – the protection of the progeny. Islam prefers people to leave their inheritors wealthy, if possible. Thus, believers are not allowed to bequeath more than one-third of the property they leave behind for charitable purposes; the remaining two-thirds have to be distributed among their heirs, including their daughters, in accordance with the Islamic law of inheritance and irrespective of their financial position. The provision is a sort of insurance to hedge against the risk of their heirs not having enough to survive on and thus having to resort to begging for survival. Allah may lengthen one's span of life for being of help to others. Modern law has moderated the insistence on insurable interest as a requirement for life insurance, and expectations now include charitable donations, among others. The change falls in line with the Islamic norm of keeping promises and may help to promote the growth of cash endowments – i.e., *waqf* – in Islamic finance. It is recognized that one may have an interest in the continued life, health, and physical fitness of another person and may risk financial loss due to that person's demise, ill health, or disability. Many employers may therefore have an insurable interest in their employees. Health and accident coverage are provided by many employers – public and private – to their employees on a selective basis, not to all. The increasing expansion of coverage under insurable interest tends to improve the welfare of a wide spectrum of wives, children, and employees. It adds to productivity and output and increases the general satisfaction of the populace. Islamic law supports such an expansion in general.

9.2.3 Indemnity

The principle of indemnity requires a guarantee or assurance from the insurer that the insured person will be recompensed or returned to the position that he/ she was in immediately before the uncertain event, which caused the damage, happened. The insurer undertakes to meet in full the actual financial loss suffered. The principle is applicable to fire, marine, and other general categories of insurance affecting material goods. In an insurance contract, the amount of compensation is limited to the amount assured or the actual losses, whichever is less. The compensation cannot be more or less than the actual damage. Compensation is not paid if the specific loss does not happen due to a particular reason or during a specific time period. The insurance contract grants protection; the policyholder cannot use it to make a profit.

9.2.4 Proximate cause

An indemnity claim must be based on reason. This means that the damage must be the result of an event covered by the contract. Any injury suffered in an unsuccessful attempt to commit suicide cannot invoke indemnity, for example, nor can setting on one's own house on fire. Compensation cannot be claimed except for the damage caused by events specified in the contract. Such causes have to be candidly specified and explained in the contract. A proximate – i.e., an immediate, not distant – cause must justify the claim.

9.2.5 Beneficiary issue

Islamic law does not permit the determination of a beneficiary in *takaful* by inserting a nominee clause in the contract. The beneficiary must have an insurable interest in the policy; the nominee may or may not have that interest. Nominees are essentially trustees, and their position is defined by the *amanah* or trusteeship rules. Again, the current practice of treating heirs as having an insurable interest in the policy is questionable, as *takaful* rules and procedures are silent on the issue.

9.2.6 Underwriting

Takaful is a risky business because it buys the risks of *others*. How much risk each *takaful* proposal carries and what premium is appropriate to cover it is difficult to assess for those with ordinary managerial skills. For this reason, insurance companies – conventional and Islamic – employ experts known as *underwriters*. Underwriters are trained and experienced professionals. Put together, these principles fix the operational framework for *takaful*. They lend weight to, and justify, the seeking of information concerning the policy takers on matters such as their age, financial status, medical fitness, legal competence, civil record, and the validity of their rights, especially in family *takaful*.

9.3 Islam and insurance

The term *takaful* comes from the Arabic root word *kafalah*, meaning responsibility or guarantee. For members of a tribe, it referred to their joint responsibility or collective guarantee. If a member of one tribe was unintentionally killed by a member of another tribe, payment of 'blood money' was the only way to stop revenge killings and even war between them. The members of the paying tribe would donate money to meet the agreed blood price, and once their contributions were made, they could not be withdrawn. The larger the tribe, the less each individual's burden. The Prophet (may peace be upon him) endorsed this pre-Islamic principle, known as *Al-aqila* because it was based on mutual help and cooperation. To illustrate, Umar bin Al-khattab, the second caliph (634–644 AD), instructed each district of the state to maintain records of every individual serving in the Muslim army so that they could contribute 'blood money' in case any of the soldiers indulged in the slaughter of the enemy's noncombatants when on military campaigns.

There is also a legend from Indian medieval history that Noor Jehan, the beloved wife of the Mughal king Alamgir, escaped capital punishment when the widow of the washman the queen had killed by mistake agreed to accept the blood money the queen had offered as compensation. Support for *takaful* in general follows from the Islamic emphasis on promoting brotherhood, solidarity, and mutual help among believers. The Qur'an instructs, "*Cling one and all to the faith of Allah and let nothing divide you*" (3:103). We shall see that it is submission to the 'right path' that makes *takaful* different from conventional insurance. And it is this submission that places wealth protection among the five leading objectives (*maqasid*) of *Shari'ah*, and gives *takaful* an exalted place in the Islamic financial system. The principle of mutual help makes people their own insurers. *Takaful* emerged not long after Islamic banking and was soon on course for expansion. In selecting a mode of operation, institutions, and instruments, the Islamic financial system has found it expedient to follow mainstream arrangements, modifying them sufficiently to comply with juristic requirements.

Takaful was developed essentially as a parallel system to mainstream insurance. Once started, *takaful* expanded fast since 2005. The average growth for the decade is 19% a year compared with 5% for conventional insurance businesses. However, this comparison of ratios is deceptive unless we know the basis on which the ratios have been calculated – e.g., 2% of 10,000 is double of 10% of 1,000. So, even though *takaful* has been the fastest-growing segment of the Islamic finance sector, its share in the assets of the system is still no more than 1%. Also, the growth of *takaful* has been patchy across regions, the major areas being Southeast Asia and Africa.

9.3.1 Takaful *versus insurance*

Takaful and conventional insurance have areas of affinity and areas of divergence. The initial principle of cooperative help, which emerged in early tribal culture as a necessary means to mitigate risk, and in the context of blood money payments, is common to both *takaful* and to the origins of conventional insurance (only later, with the establishment of insurance companies, did they begin to diverge). So too is the prerequisite of insurable interest. Actuarial risk measurement techniques for premium determination are also common to both. Nor do the types of documentation, forms, and procedures differ that much. But beyond these similarities, *takaful* differs from conventional insurance on numerous counts. The main ones are as follows:

1 *Takaful* is based on the principle of mutual help and cooperation while conventional insurance quickly became a purely commercial proposition. The spirit behind the two is quite different. In *takaful*, all or part of the contribution paid by the participant is a donation (*tabarru*) to the *takaful* fund, which helps participants provide protection to each other against potential risks. There is complete segregation between the participants' *takaful* fund accounts and the company shareholders' accounts. In contrast, conventional insurance is an outright sales contract, wherein the premium that policyholders pay to the company is in *exchange* for the protection provided from the underwritten risk. Premium payments generate income for the company's shareholders to enable risk-taking.

2 *Takaful* is free from interest (*riba*), gambling (*maysir*), and uncertainty (*gharar*); conventional insurance does not exclude these elements from its operations. It may be added that *takaful*, despite all precautions,

may still contain some element of *gharar*, but it is treated as tolerable because of the other distinguishing features of the contract. In conventional insurance, all surpluses and profits belong to the shareholders of the company. In contrast, any surplus in the *takaful* fund is to be shared mostly by the participants, and the investment profits are distributed among the participants and the shareholders, depending on the choice of model (see the following section). If a participant's contribution to the fund is in deficit, a participant may receive an interest-free loan (*qard hasan*) from the *takaful* fund operator, whereas in conventional insurance, the operator company covers only the risks.

3   The participants' contribution and the shareholders' capital are invested in funds that are *Shari'ah*-compliant. In conventional insurance, the premium received is invested in securities and funds that are not necessarily *Shari'ah* compliant: no distinction is made between *haram* and *halal* investment channels. Making that distinction is obligatory in *takaful*; what is unlawful has to be avoided.

9.3.2 Forms of takaful

Like conventional insurance, we have two forms of *takaful* as well: general and family. Conventional life insurance is replaced within family *takaful* for reasons we have already explained. *General takaful* schemes are basically contracts of joint guarantee, on a short-term basis – normally one year – between participants to provide mutual compensation should a defined material loss take place. For example, the house of a group member is damaged in a fire, his car is stolen, the ship carrying his goods sinks on the high seas, or he suffers physical injuries in an accident. In all such cases, the suffering member may need finance to remedy the damage. General *takaful* is *taawun* – i.e., cooperation for mutual help to restore the house of a group member, replace his stolen car or destroyed merchandise, or cover medical expenses for the treatment of the injuries he suffered in the accident.

For receiving help in such exigencies, the participating individuals in the various *takaful* schemes agree to pay *takaful* contributions to the company that manages the general *takaful* business. The contribution constitutes a fund, and the money is invested in *Shari'ah*-compliant assets and businesses to generate income. The investment function is performed by the same *takaful* company that receives the contributions. The company operates as a *mudharib* (entrepreneur) in the matter and invests the general *takaful* fund in *halal* lines of business. Returns on investment are pooled back to strengthen the fund. The company pays compensation or indemnity to fellow participants who have suffered a defined loss upon the occurrence of a harmful event from this general fund. The fund is also used to meet other operational costs of the business and for setting up special purpose reserves if needed.

If the general *takaful* fund shows a surplus after all its operational costs have been met in full, the surplus is distributed among the participants and the company, provided the participants have not incurred any claims and that no compensations have been paid to them. This sharing of the surplus will be in a ratio agreed upon in accordance with the contract of *Al-Mudarabah*. If the agreed ratio is 1:1, then the participants and the company owners would each have 50% of the disposable surplus.

In contrast, family *takaful* involves long-term risk coverage, say from 10 to 30 years. Here, most of the policy takers are saving for their distant needs, such as for health care, the education of their children, housing, providing an income in retirement, or leaving an inheritance for their heirs in some measure. Family *takaful* companies generally divide participants' contributions (in the premium form) into their (i) savings accounts and (ii) special (*tabarru*) accounts. The latter accounts are meant to meet the losses of *takaful* participants, according to pre-agreed terms. Thus, a *tabarru* clause in the individual contracts is inserted to record this agreement. The savings part is invested in income-earning projects, and the company may share these profits with the policyholders, depending on the terms of the contract. On the other hand, *tabarru* is reserved for meeting the compensation claims falling due under individual contracts. We will discuss these accounts in more detail in the next section. In general *takaful*, participants' contributions are not divided in this way; the whole fund operates as *tabarru*. Family *takaful* has two broad categories: (i) ordinary or individual family *takaful* or (ii) group family *takaful*. Under the ordinary type, the individual policy may provide cover for education, health, travel, a family savings plan, and *waqf* (endowment) for financial assistance in the event of death or permanent disability. Long-term savings and investment profits distributed upon a claim, maturity, or on premature surrender of the plan may also be available. Employers, clubs, associations, cooperatives, and societies may seek group family *takaful* for their members. *Takaful* companies welcome this sort of business because it requires a minimum number of participants and thus guarantees a certain pot of funds. It is a profitable business. Group family *takaful* plans involve cover for education, health, travel, etc., for the members of the group. Participants receive financial benefits in the event of death or permanent disability. Annuity plans providing regular incomes and investment-linked policies are also available to the participants.

9.4 *Takaful*: Illustrative models

9.4.1 *Mudarabah model*

We have identified two broad categories of *takaful* – family and general. These categories are mutually exclusive but the contracts they use are not. The same contract structure is used for each category; it is simply the application that is different. Thus, one must take care in explaining the structure of a contract to clarify which category type – family or general – one is

118   Islam and insurance (takaful)

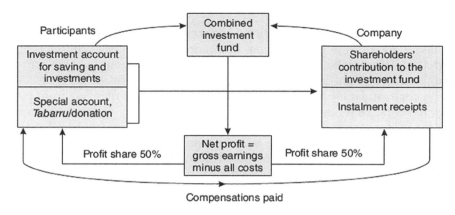

Figure 9.1 Mudarabah model in family takaful.

talking about. Islamic law allows a variety of contracts to accommodate the diverse needs of the participants and operators engaged in *takaful* business. Figure 9.1 specifies the basic form of the family *takaful* contract and its operational elements. It is important to choose an appropriate type of contract that matches the peculiarities of each *takaful* proposal. The operators must ensure *Shari'ah* compliance of the selected form. In this context, they need to have in place procedures and policies that can sustain a business over the long term and also balance the conflicting interests of the various stakeholders – the owners of the company, the insured, and society in general. Keeping in view the technical, regional, and regulatory aspects of the business and the targeted population may help to make this task easier.

9.4.2 The waqf model

The *waqf* approach for organizing *takaful* business is of recent origin and is not in common use. South Africa and a few other countries use it to meet some socio-legal demands. The operator or company initiates a *waqf* account in the *takaful* fund, which itself provides some seed money for the purpose. The payments that participants make to obtain the cover are credited to this account, which is then operated in accordance with the principles of *waqf*, or endowment, to achieve the following objectives: (a) to provide financial assistance to individual members when losses do take place and (b) to arrange benefits to its members strictly according to the letter and spirit of the *waqf* deed.

In the *waqf* model, the company performs all the needed functions of the *waqf* as the agent for a *wakalah* fee, which it deducts from the contributions paid by the participants. This includes all the underwriting expenses and *takaful* costs – nothing is normally charged to the w*aqf* fund. The funds, net of agency fees, are invested. The gross amount minus investment and fund

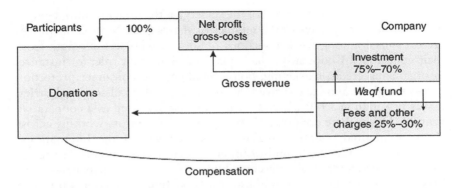

Figure 9.2 Operational framework in waqf takaful.

management costs is given in total (100%) to the participants. Likewise, all surpluses in the *takaful* fund, after paying compensations, go to the participants. Thus seen, the model is of a hybrid sort – a mixture of *waqf* and *wakalah*.

As mentioned earlier, the *waqf* model is not in much use and came into being as a socio-legal imperative. Also, *waqf* is a rather rigid structure to form the basis of a business venture like *takaful*. The term *waqf* refers to a faith-oriented endowment. It entails a voluntary and irrevocable commitment of one's wealth –in full or in part – in cash or in kind (such as a mill or a garden), and for use in *hari'ah* compliant projects (such as a mosque school or a graveyard).

Waqf is a permanent donation; once created, it can never be undone or given as a gift, or inherited, or sold. The person providing the endowment can determine which sources are used to generate income. The crucial feature of the model is that the creator of the *waqf* fund decides the rules for the distribution of its proceeds to beneficiaries and determines how much compensation will be paid out to a participant. Impartial observance of these norms is difficult because the operator of the fund is both its manager and functions at the same time as the *mudarib* or entrepreneur. There can be a clash of interests in performing the dual role. Figure 9.2 presents the structure of a waqf model.

9.4.3 Cooperatives

Since *takaful* has grown and thrived on the Islamic notion of mutual help and *ummatic* (communal) unity, its organization along the lines of the cooperative society model is often urged. The motto of the cooperative movement is "*each for all and all for each*". A cooperative is a form of business organization that is established, managed, and operated by a group of people to promote their common interests. Each member contributes equity capital and shares in the control of the society on the principle of one-member, one-vote, irrespective of the number of shares held. Most cooperatives are organized among weaker sections of society, who seek strength from their collectivity. Cooperatives have played a significant role, for instance, in organizing credit, marketing, house-building, and consumer protection across the globe and have thrived in agriculture and small-scale industries. It was in Sudan in 1979 where *takaful* was first launched as a cooperative venture. Today, there are presently many *takaful* operators working across about a hundred countries registered as members of the International Cooperative and Mutual Fund Insurance Federation – a nonprofit organization. The cooperative obtains contributions from the participants – members and nonmembers – to establish a *takaful* fund. The cooperative can use any of the aforementioned models, or any combination of them, to run its business.

Cooperatives cannot make much headway in *takaful* business for a variety of reasons, including paucity of funds and lack of managerial skills. Above all, cooperation is not just business; it is a culture. Unless cooperation begins at the heart – i.e., one really has the cooperative spirit – it can rarely hope to succeed.

9.5 Risk valuation

Insurance is one business that deals only in risks. Averages and probabilities provide the foundation on which the insurance structure rests. This obviously makes the structure fragile. *Takaful* includes the essential features of conventional insurance but is constrained by *Shari'ah* norms. Observation of these norms creates additional risks for a *takaful* business. The highly risky nature of the business of insurance – conventional or Islamic – demands special precautions regarding the mobilization of financial resources, the treatment of risk, and the pricing of insurance products.

A brief explanation of the demands follows. In insurance, all expenses relating to the operational management of the chosen model are the responsibility of the operator. The business is inherently open to fluctuations: the number of compensatory claims may fluctuate unpredictably for a variety of reasons. If the *takaful* fund is unable to meet current or future obligations, the operator may be declared insolvent. Also, the returns on investments may not be sufficient to keep the participants happy.

The ability of the operator to escape such adverse consequences depends on the fund remaining in surplus. The volume of surplus grows over time in the form of the accumulated retention of participants' contributions and the profits being in excess of payments to settle claims. The distribution of money from the surplus to the participants is controlled. It is vital to keep assets sufficiently liquid in case there are abnormal claims and to absorb shocks. The matching of assets and liabilities may be an accounting necessity but is not a condition sufficient for survival. The financial

Islam and insurance (takaful) 121

responsibilities and the precarious nature of risk in *takaful* tend to make the process of product pricing complicated and cautious. To begin with, product pricing requires the collection of data, for example on mortality rates, the frequency of accidents and their causes, claims distribution, participants' withdrawal patterns, and so on. Assumptions about the market environment, the state of the competition, and rivals' reactions need to be assessed. Other information, including government fiscal policy and regulatory measures, also need to be considered. Expenditure on documentation, the processing of applications, as well as on marketing and publicity has to be estimated. Pricing decisions in *takaful* require an element of value judgment as much as objectivity. This fact has led to calls for closer regulatory supervision in the interest of both the participants and the operators. Regulation focuses on the *capital assets ratio*. As *takaful* companies work on the same patterns as mainstream insurance companies, the notion of *risk-based capital* in the conventional regulatory framework covers *takaful* as well. This framework allows *re-takaful*.

9.5.1 Re-takaful

Parallel to re-insurance in the conventional system, we have re-*takaful* in Islamic finance, although the two are not identical. Re-*takaful* can be better understood if defined as "*takaful* for *takaful* operators", that is taking out a *takaful* policy for *takaful* policies. A parent *takaful* company piles up risks as the number of policies it sells increases. At some stage of growth, the company may fear that the covering of liabilities associated with the accumulated risks may be difficult to meet or that it may possibly experience financial hardship if a large group of claims happened to mature at the same time, as happened, for example, in the aftermath of natural disasters like the tsunami in 2004. The company sees a way to reduce its risks by taking out a re-*takaful* policy with another company to cover part of the risks it carries. Broadly, two methods are in current use for re-*takaful*: (i) the facultative method and (ii) the treaty method. Under facultative re-*takaful*, a contract is negotiated for a specific, individual *takaful* policy. This type is purchased when the policy is unusual or large and the original operator is concerned about liability risks. The policyholder is not informed about re-*takaful*. In contrast, under the treaty method, a group of policies or risk categories is covered together by a single re-*takaful* company. There are other reasons too for seeking re-*takaful*. It enables the decant to move out of a business category or region or production line through transference to a re-*takaful* company. *Takaful* operators have the opportunity to spread risk on new lines of business until the fund magnitude attains a certain maturity level. Re-*takaful* may serve as a source of information on underwriting when going into a new line of business or a new market. It helps ease the strain on the cedent's capital during periods of high contribution growth. Re-*takaful* is a relatively new business area in the field of Islamic

122   Islam and insurance (takaful)

finance and its growth was slow until 2005 when most *takaful* companies approached conventional operators for re-*takaful*. The Shari'ah Advisory Council temporarily allowed the practice as a *darura* (necessity) until the proper Islamic re-*takaful* facilities expand sufficiently to meet the Islamic requirements.

9.6 Summary

- Uncertainty makes the outcome of current action unpredictable. It can be favorable or unfavorable to the decision-maker. Thus, uncertainty creates the risk of decisions going wrong and can result in financial losses.
- Some of the risks that uncertainty generates can be statistically measured while others cannot be measured. Risks that can be measured can be met at a cost. Insurance companies – conventional and Islamic – take on these risks from each other in return for payments. We call this re-insurance or re-*takaful*. Insurance is thus a big business.
- In its modern shape, insurance emerged as a protection against damage caused by fire and was first to appear in Britain. Insurance against the loss of goods through plunder, pilferage, or because a ship had sunk on the high seas followed next. Soon life insurance joined the list, and the insurance industry expanded fast.
- Insurance is a very risky venture because it is the only business where nothing but risk is the stock in trade. Therefore, it operates on some unique principles to minimize the owners' risks arising from getting transferred to self the risks of others to earn returns on shareholders' equity. So, operators and the insurance seekers both have to scrupulously observe certain well-laid-out principles.
- Among the principles, two deserve special mention: utmost good faith and the proof of insurable interest. The nature of the insurance contract requires the parties to the contract to be transparent and provide all information that can help the other in making well-informed decisions. The contract requires honesty and utmost good faith by all parties.
- Proof that the beneficiary named under the policy has a genuine insurable interest in the coverage of the risk for which the policy has been taken is vital. There must be evidence that the beneficiary would suffer a loss financially or emotionally before a contract can be signed.
- The concept of insurance or protection from danger (risk) is special to Islam and is supported by a historical and cultural legacy rooted in tribal living and the spirit of mutual help. However, its modern form is of much later vintage and started in Sudan.
- Islamic insurance endorses and accommodates many features of conventional insurance but it is not a carbon copy. The primary differences arise from the Islamic ban on interest and avoiding indeterminacy and speculation when entering into the contract. *Takaful* engages in *halal*

activities alone. There are other differences as well. To distinguish it from conventional insurance it has assumed an Arabic nomenclature – *takaful*.

- Like conventional insurance, there are also two types of *takaful*: general and family. The latter's further divided into two subcategories: individual family *takaful* and group family *takaful*.
- Islam allows a variety of *takaful* contracts to accommodate the diverse interests of the participants and the operators. The major ones include *wakalah*, *mudarabah* and *waqf*. Variations can be created through combinations of the main forms. A *jua'lah* clause may be added to enhance the commission of the operator to a reasonable level.
- The *waqf* model is usually combined with other models to overcome its limitations. Despite this, it is not much in use because of these practical limitations. This is also the case with the usage of cooperatives to promote *takaful*.
- Selection of an appropriate model or creating a hybrid model is important in conducting *takaful* business. For this reason, the selection of models and their operational features differ across countries.
- Financial risks and the pricing of *takaful* products are intimately related. Pricing is thus a difficult subject in *takaful*.

Chapter 10

Law regulation and governance

Chapter contents

- Islamic Finance: diverse theory and practice across countries
- Common law, civil law, and *Shari'ah*
- Regulatory issues and standards
- Liquidity-profit trade-off: issue and solution
- Basel Accords and Islamic finance
- Governance: problems and challenges

The observance of *Shari'ah* norms makes Islamic financial institutions, operation modes, and instruments much different from mainstream systems. Thus, Islamic institutions cannot do what the mainstream can and does. Likewise, mainstream institutions are not obliged to do what Islam demands. Yet, Islamic institutions must operate in an environment that confronts them with common and civil laws of the secular vintage both at home and abroad. Adjustment and reconciliation are serious challenges. To face them, *Shari'ah* frameworks are developed and updated. This chapter takes stock of these and related developments.

10.1 Introduction

This chapter introduces the reader to a wide range of issues in Islamic finance relating to legal provisions, regulatory frameworks, and corporate governance problems. We shall provide a broad treatment of the selected topics without going into their finer details or the controversies they provoke. Rather, we shall focus on aspects of the current position from the Islamic financial institutions' perspective.

DOI: 10.4324/9781003366973-10

10.1.1 Dominance of diversity

The governance of financial institutions – secular or Islamic – requires a legal framework containing its principles and rules of conduct. How these legal systems come into existence in each case is different. Secular law is the result of domestic legislative action followed by its juridical interpretations. The same procedures that bring it into existence can repeal or amend it. In contrast, Islamic law (*Shari'ah*) is God ordained. It is derived from the Islamic sources of knowledge, mainly the scripture and the Prophetic traditions. The derivation results from the interpretation of the sources. Thus, Islamic financial law is juridical. Here, the law contained in the sources follows their interpretation. Thus, we have four major Sunni schools of jurisprudence with divisions within, in addition to the Shiite. The multiplicity of interpretations lends to infirmity in application; differences need to be narrowed.

This diversity has caused the prevalent complexity of products and procedures across countries and hinders the internationalization of the Islamic system and the development of global markets for its products. A need for the standardization of Islamic contracts and practices is frequently voiced as the way to overcome the difficulties created by the current diversity in the interpretation and application of Islamic provisions, which are blocking the way to progress. Efforts in that direction are being made, and more are expected to follow in due course. However, worrying too much about the variations in the contracts across jurisdictions or about the merits of different practices also carries the risk of sharpening juristic divisions, and these may be just as detrimental to the healthy and rapid growth of the industry in the years ahead. Efforts to achieve a perceived uniformity cannot ignore the fact that diversity has, in some measure, positive and helpful implications as well.

The Qur'an emphasizes flexibility and accommodation as a hallmark of the principles that govern human life: "*Allah does not want to place you in difficulty, but to make you clean and complete His favors on you so that you may be grateful*". (5: 5–6) Thus, there are instructions in the Qur'an to allow a debtor who is experiencing difficulties time to repay the loan, and it is all the more commendable if the lender foregoes the claim by way of charity (2: 280). The Prophet (peace be upon him) allowed people to take the easier course provided all of the options were *Shari'ah* compliant. Variations impart flexibility to the system: they allow the forging of instruments and models over a wider range of time and space. The peaceful coexistence of multiple schools of thought and their subtle differences in Islamic jurisprudence through the ages testifies to the pragmatic wisdom that diversity embodies.

Unity in diversity has been the hallmark of Islamic glory throughout most of its history. The demand for uniformity in juristic positions possibly underpins the drift of the Islamic financial system toward convergence with conventional norms and practices. It is perhaps time for the unidirectional convergence of the systems to end and to see movement from the other direction as well. Western financial laws and practices have yet to take steps in that direction: Islamic financial practices have perhaps been left with little scope but to go with the flow. The Islamic system has an ethical commitment and a social welfare dimension; it is not solely concerned with the maximization of pecuniary gains for the stakeholders. Its program is much wider than the confines of other social systems.

It is surprising that despite all the ease and flexibility that the Islamic system allows, the bulk of the Muslim population remains detached from its benefits. The total financial assets the system owns at present in Muslim-majority countries are less than 20%, although country differences are quite wide. The popularity of Islamic finance is on the rise. The industry, including banking, funds, and insurance, has been growing at an average annual rate of over 3% since 2017 and is estimated to cross the $3.69 trillion mark in 2024

There are three areas of Islamic finance which are closely interrelated: law, regulation, and governance. The diversities within and between them differ in content, form, and impact depending on the nature of the procedures involved. For instance, a financial contract is drafted, as in conventional finance, by an advocate working for a law firm or with an Islamic financial institution. The document defines the terms and conditions concerning the subject matter of the contract and specifies the reciprocal considerations and the mode of their discharge. It also spells out the consequences of the breach of contract from either of the parties. Despite the checkered history of its evolution, Islamic finance presents significant new business opportunities and provides alternative methods for capital formation and economic development across countries without distinction, especially regarding its relationship with common law and civil law. Let us explain this distinction to understand better what follows.

10.1.2 Law and Islamic finance

Despite the checkered history of its evolution, Islamic finance presents significant new business opportunities and provides alternative methods for capital formation and economic development across countries without distinction, especially regarding its relationship with common law and civil law. Let us explain this distinction so we can better understand the following discussion.

Common law is based on the ancient historical legacy of England. It has its origin in societal customs and the court judgments that have been delivered over the centuries. The law is uniformly applied without distinction. It was also influenced by Islamic tribal customs during the period when Muslims ruled over part of Europe, especially in Spain and Sicily. Many countries like Australia, the United Kingdom, Germany, and the United States have over time incorporated English common law into their legal systems. Civil law, on the other hand, can be traced back to the Roman legal system, although its modern form is a much more recent development. Thus, whereas common law is based on custom, civil law is statutory in nature. It basically deals with the rights and responsibilities of private, individual citizens. The two legal systems – common and civil – operate side by side in harmony with one another.

Islamic *Shari'ah* accommodates custom, or *urf*, as it is called, in the dispensation of justice, so in some respects it seems closer to common law. However, it is different from both common and civil law on several counts. Whereas both types of law are man-made, *Shari'ah* is divine. Civil law is an expression of the majority will in a democratic country. The majority can change or even repeal its laws. *Shari'ah* provisions are God ordained; they are unalterable. Only their interpretations can change, but that too is within limits. This creates scope for *ijtihad*, or reinterpretation. It imparts a measured flexibility to the system. Law deals essentially with objective, specifiable consequences of disputes that are factual in content; it rarely accommodates ethical values and moral norms, which are the distinctive features of the *Shari'ah*. In this respect, the commonly used expression 'Shari'ah law' seems to suffer from an internal inconsistency. Islamic finance surfaced as part of the Islamic resurgent movements when most of the Muslim world was still under colonial rule. There was no question of Islamic norms and values having any place in the legal system of the occupied lands. In the second half of the twentieth century, the shackles started to loosen, and by the 1960s, most of the Muslim countries across the world had won independence from foreign rule. However, independent boundaries did not always ensure freedom in choosing policies. The hangover of the colonial era on social infrastructure, attitudinal frames, internal squabbles, and the sweep of the global demands by the ex-rulers slowed the pace of and muffled the directions of Islamic revivalism. The secular laws for businesses, including finance, were already in place in Muslim countries but opinion was divided on how they should be interpreted – what, indeed, was Islamic or un-Islamic in those laws. This added to the diversity of legal frameworks for Islamic finance in Muslim countries. Only Sudan and Iran have a unifying Islamic law covering all financial institutions. In Pakistan, a blueprint for an Islamic banking system was commissioned but was never enacted. Currently, the country runs a parallel regime – it has fully-fledged Islamic banks and allows Islamic windows in mainstream conventional banks. There is no separate law covering Islamic financial services. Malaysia was sailing in the same boat before it put into operation a separating Islamic Banking Services Act in May 2013. It no longer allows the opening of Islamic windows in conventional banks, although the older ones have survived. Other Muslim countries, for example, Libya, Algeria, Tunisia, and Turkey, and countries in Central Asia have no exclusive laws for Islamic finance. However, the thinking seems to be changing. In 2011, the African Development Bank reported that at least 30 countries have either enacted separate banking laws for Islamic banks or inserted special provisions for them in their existing laws. In Middle East countries like Saudi Arabia, which do not have separate Islamic banking laws, the same may soon emerge. In Turkey, where Islamic banks are known as *participation banks*, change is picking up pace. Islamic finance is also making inroads in new areas, including in the so far untouched corners of Africa and the Central Asian nations, where the prospects for Islamic banking are brightening. The Islamic Development Bank is making concerted efforts to encourage the introduction of Islamic finance in Central Asia, especially for agriculture and rural housing.

Outside the Muslim world, places like London, Paris, and Luxembourg are fast emerging as new centers of Islamic finance. However, Islamic financial institutions in such places operate under secular laws, without any special provisions for the Islamic system. Both in Europe and America, courts are protective of the financial aims of the contract and do not accept *Shari'ah*-based defenses that undermine the validity of the agreement. Nevertheless, where the confines of the contract are in question, the courts are willing to engage in independent reasoning based on sources of Islamic jurisprudence. This is also the case in places such as Singapore and Hong Kong. Here, people have a fairer understanding of the faith and the legal provisions needed to boost Islamic faineance, but a law separating Islamic financial institutions from conventional ones is not in sight.

Running the Islamic financial institutions (IFIs) in parallel to the conventional ones in a competitive, dual system limits the policy options of the former in many ways. Islamic institutions have to fall into line with global standards, and there is psychological pressure for them to look like conventional institutions in their attitudes, goals, and methods of business. They also remain conscious of their Western ratings, but these may not always be fair for a variety of reasons. All this is difficult to escape from, bearing in mind that the IFIs initially opted to follow the conventional system, and now it is no longer advisable to reverse this choice. However, some of its consequences are worth noting: Islamic finance emphasizes profit-and-risk sharing as its principal point of departure from the conventional system, and its superiority on various counts flows from this distinction. However, its debt-based transactions overwhelmingly surpass real profit-and-risk-sharing contracts in number and volume despite efforts to correct the situation. The dominance of debt-based transactions has given rise to a situation where the bulk of the deposits in Islamic banks are of short-term duration; even in leading Muslim countries, long-term investment deposits are more often placed with conventional banks, not Islamic ones. However, there *are* ways in which to conduct Islamic finance outside the conventional system and within the ambit of the current legal scenario.

10.2 Need for regulations

Rules have been made for regulating the conduct of IFIs to maintain and strengthen the protective firewall. These regulatory rules have to harmonize with the legal structure of a country. Thus, the authorities framing the financial regulations and specifying their operational range differ between Muslim and non-Muslim countries, although the differences are narrowing within these groups or areas. As a minimal requirement, the national and international regulators both have to ensure that the basic financial principles of the *Shari'ah* are observed. Briefly, these include a ban on interest, the avoidance of uncertainty, adherence to risk-sharing, the promotion of ethical investment, a commitment to societal well-being, and ensuring that every commercial transaction is backed by real assets.

During the period 1950–2000, the world was awash with notions of globalization, liberalization, and privatization. Protective barriers were pulled down and deregulation was on its triumphant march. The surge in the movement of goods, labor, and capital across national borders was unprecedented, even taking in its stride the collapse of the Berlin Wall and of communism in Europe. An epoch of prosperity was ushered in across the globe, with the exception of a few dusty corners. During those 50 years, the world produced more goods and services than it had produced in its entire existence before 1950.

However, cracks in the mosaic of prosperity had already started to develop, and they soon became worrisome. Although globalization did hasten the pace of economic development, it also helped to spread the financial crises across national borders. These crises took little time to become more frequent, deeper, and more prolonged. The turmoil of the 2007 sub-prime debacle started in the USA, but the contagion spread to almost every corner of the globe. It pulled down mighty banks, insurance companies, and funds, even governments. The literature on the causes of the crisis and the economic consequences of the financial dislocations it introduced is voluminous and has led to a reversal in thought and policy on the issue of regulation.

The era of deregulation has ended. Concern has shifted back toward regulating the conduct (i.e., the procedures and practices) of financial institutions. Ensuring the safety of deposits and bank solvency are now important issues to be dealt with. The role of the central banks in regulating credit and forging counter-cyclical measures are the key issues currently under the microscope. The focal point of the reforms is how to bring ethical norms and societal welfare to the fore in the conduct of business and as the rudders steering the financial system. Indeed, writers in the area have seized upon this aspect to highlight the moral and ethical distinction of the Islamic system and its superiority over the conventional system. It is claimed that IFIs have better absorbed the crisis shocks. Such claims have an element of truth: there is empirical evidence that IFIs have been less affected by the crisis.

130 Law regulation and governance

However, sober evaluations of the ethical distinctions of Islamic finance have started to emerge. For instance, in a lecture at INCEIF in April 2013, Professor Volker Nienhaus compared the performance of Islamic finance with the conventional system with reference to observance of ethical norms as a measure of socially responsible behavior. He argued that the Islamic system incorporates units, instruments, procedures, and transactions ethical norms derived from faith; the conventional system acquires them from rational morality norms endorsed by the majority of people through democratic institutions. By implication, he made the point that having ethical norms carries no distinction for religion; secular societies are not without such norms. The distinction lies in the source of each, not in the presence and absence of ethical norms. This cannot be disputed. Notable is that practice differs from theory in both cases, presumably, more in the conventional system.

10.3 *Shari'ah*-based framework

We have seen above that IFIs operate under a two-tier legal structure – mainstream and Islamic. The infrastructure for the regulation and supervision of these institutions is organized under this two-tier legal structure. The system broadly has three layers.

First, there is the International Islamic Fiqh Academy (IIFA), established in February 1988 at Jeddah, Saudi Arabia, pursuant to a 1974 decision of the organization of Islamic countries. The main objectives of the Academy include minimizing the differences in instruments, contracts, and procedures in the area of Islamic finance. The IIFA is an institution for the advanced study of Islam. It issues rulings on various aspects of the religion, including economic aspects. However, its rulings are not binding on member countries because there are interpretational differences among the main schools of Islamic jurisprudence.

Such differences have caused the creation of national *fiqh* boards or councils. The local juristic

Organizations do not need to and do not always endorse the edicts issued by the IIFA. To illustrate, the Academy does not approve the use of *inah* and organized *tawarruq* in Islamic finance, while the National *Shari'ah* Council of Malaysia at Bank Negara does allow them.

The second layer is the Islamic Finance Services Board (IFSB). The board is a high-powered international standard-setting organization. It came into existence in 2003 and is located at Kuala Lumpur, Malaysia. The governing council of the IFSB is presently composed of central bank governors from 20 Muslim countries. The board aims at promoting and enhancing the soundness and stability of Islamic financial services by issuing global standards of financial prudence and guiding principles for the industry in banking, capital markets, and *takaful*.

The standards prepared by the IFSB follow a lengthy process that involves, *inter alia*, issuing exposure drafts, holding workshops, and, where necessary, arranging public hearings. The IFSB also conducts research and coordinates initiatives on industry-related issues as well as organizing roundtables, seminars, and conferences for regulators and industry stakeholders. Toward this end, the IFSB works closely with relevant international, regional, and national organizations, research and educational institutions, and market players.

The third layer comprises the Accounting and Auditing Organization for Islamic Financial Institutions (AAOIFI). It was founded in 1991 and is based in Bahrain. Some leading jurists, central banks, IFIs, and other bodies in the industry are among its 200 members from 45 countries. It periodically issues international Standards on *Shari'ah* Accounting, Auditing, and Corporate Governance for IFIs. Many leading Islamic finance centers around the world have adopted its regulatory standards. The AAOIFI and IFSB proposals are having a visible impact on the regulatory framework of the IFIs. For example, banks now invariably establish *Shari'ah*

Supervisory Boards and ensure their independence. The memorandum of agreement and articles of association of each Islamic bank specify how its *Shari'ah* Supervisory Board will be established and what its composition, powers, and decision-making procedures will be. Thus, in Kuwait, for example, each Islamic bank must have such a board consisting of at least three members appointed by its general assembly. The board has to prepare an annual report containing its opinions of the bank's operations. The report has to be submitted to the general assembly of shareholders and published in the Bank's annual report.

Outside the Muslim world, the United Kingdom has shown more interest in Islamic finance than many other countries, perhaps partly because London has long been the leading financial center of the world and the United Kingdom wants to maintain that position in the newly emerging sector of international finance. Even though the United Kingdom has no separate legislation for accommodating Islamic finance, its Financial Services and Markets Act 2000 provides for the registration of IFIs. To do so, the following requirements must be met:

- An Islamic financial institution must be incorporated as a company in the United Kingdom and must have its head office and senior management located in the United Kingdom.
- It must have adequate resources for the business it proposes to conduct and its management has to be sufficiently skillful to work independently in an appropriate manner.
- The applicant institution must satisfy the Financial Services Authority (FSA) about the efficacy of the products before launching the proposed business to enable the authorities to determine the appropriate regulatory requirements.
- The FSA, being a secular organization, does not know and does not need to know whether the service provided is or is not *Shari'ah*-compliant,

132 Law regulation and governance

but in order to ensure customer protection it needs to know if there is a creditable system in place to monitor the IFI's compliance in terms of its specified definition. This would, for example, require the service provider to appoint a *Shari'ah*

Supervisory Board and to monitor how such supervision affects the services. In the USA, the Federal Banking Regulators provide formal guidance about the Islamic financial products through the Office of Currency Comptroller (OCC). The office has so far issued two directives on *Shari'ah*-compliant mortgages

1   It issued guidelines on *ijara* (leasing) in 1997. We have seen that in this contract the financial intermediary, such as a bank, purchases an asset – say a house, a car, or a computer – and leases it to a client for a periodic fee or rent.
2   In 1999, the OCC granted recognition to *murabahah* – a cost-plus financial structure that Islam allows in trading. Here, the financier (or bank) buys an asset for the client on the understanding that the client will buy it back for a higher (cost +) price.
3   Islamic assets come into existence as a result of *Shari'ah*-compliant investment; they are ethical for the believers.

Of late, the USA's interest in Islamic finance seems to be growing, possibly as much for political reasons as for economic ones. The UN sanctions against countries like Iran may probably work more effectively

10.3.1 Illustration – Malaysia

It is noteworthy that Malaysia has enacted this year two companion pieces of legislation (i) the Financial Services Act 2013 (FSA) and (ii) the Islamic Financial Services Act 2013 (IFSA) for streamlining its financial regulatory system. Together, the Acts carry far-reaching implications for the Islamic financial system. Put briefly, the main ones are as follows.

*   The financial holding companies – Islamic or conventional – have to observe the new regulation. However, they have the choice to stay out of their ambit if they cut down their stakes in parent financial institutions to below 50% (for individuals, the limit is 10%). They also have to allocate more resources to improve any weaknesses in internal controls
*   Bank Negara Malaysia (BNM) approval is needed for the appointment of the chairman, director, and chief executive officer of the bank. The person must fulfill the requirements stated in the Act(s) and as specified by the BNM.

- Insurance companies holding composite licenses can no longer carry on both the life insurance/and general insurance business together. The separation of businesses rule applies to Takaful companies as well.
- The affected banks must comply with the regulations not later than five years from the date of implementation of the Act(s) or longer as specified by the Minister of Finance, on the recommendation of BNM. Failure may attract penalties.

10.3.2 Key issues

The foregoing discussion provides the overall approach for dealing with the regulatory issues from the *Shari'ah* viewpoint. There is a host of such issues, but in this book, we will restrict the discussion to some of the main ones, including the following:

a   *Shari'ah* norms for identifying the companies that are engaged in permissible or *halal* businesses. This is crucial for the allocation of Islamic deposits and funds that are available for gainful investment.
b   The use of *inah* and *tawarruq* in Islamic finance because the debate on the point has divided product designs, contract structures, and modes of financing across countries and regions. The discussion will present both sides of the divide without taking positions.
c   As Islamic finance is a part of the overall global system operating parallel to conventional institutions, the international changes in the regulatory rules cannot be ignored. Thus, the broad features of the Basel declarations I, II, and III will be explained.

10.3.3 Shari'ah *screening*

Shari'ah screening broadly involves three stages. First, one has to identify the industries where the *Shari'ah* screen is the process of ascertaining the juristic requirements a company stocks. We have already discussed stock screening in Chapter 9. Here, we summarize and illustrate that discussion. *Shari'ah* screening broadly involves three stages. First, the industries that do not meet Islamic requirements at all are identified. These include companies that are engaged in such activities as the production of pork, alcohol, or pornography, or those that are engaged in gambling. The companies in other industries are then considered for screening so that a *Shari'ah*-based stock index, like the Dow Jones, can be constructed. In the second stage, there are a vast array of businesses where there can be a mix of permissible (*halal*) and prohibited activities. This presents a testing ground for the regulators. The jurists have to agree upon the tolerable proportions of *haram* in the mix. Even when this hurdle has been overcome, the third step is to determine which of the remaining mix qualifies for Islamic investment and which does not.

134 Law regulation and governance

Further difficulties arise in this third and final stage – the screening of individual firms. Business activity is dynamic, so what qualifies as *halal* business today may possibly violate the various qualifying ratios tomorrow. In modern businesses, acquisitions, mergers, and expansions are on the rise, especially due to recurring financial crises. Constant vigilance is required. Still, lapses from prescribed norms may not be rare, because the *Shari'ah* screening methodology is based on the *ijtihad* (Islamic legal reasoning) of the *Shari'ah* scholars. There are no Islamic legal texts referring to any benchmarks of *Shari'ah* compliance for company stocks. With this description of the overall scenario in mind, let us now consider some of the specific areas that are usually identified.

10.3.3.1 Capital adequacy

Banking is an attractive business because of the profits it promises for the owners, but it is also a risky business. The objective of regulations and supervision is, of course, to see that banks are observant of Islamic norms in conducting their activities, but equally, if not more importantly, their objective is to restrain the financial institutions from indulging in over-risky ventures. Supervisors must have a deep knowledge of the risks relating to investment depositors. These include risks relating to *Shari'ah* compliance, civil courts' intervention, market fluctuations, and so on. In finance, regulation and supervision essentially centers on risk treatment, not only for the overall system but also for individual institutions. The mounting and colossal failures of financial institutions – banks, insurance companies, and funds – in the wake of the 2007–2008 financial crisis caused an "issue shift", so to speak, in economics: the yesteryear advocates of liberalization and privatization turned, almost overnight, into loud proponents for raising the existing safety walls around the interests of various stakeholders, especially depositors, in the financial services sector.

There is ample evidence to show that the lure of leverage gains has led financial institutions to expand credit beyond what the volume and quality of their capital assets can support without crossing the limits of safety. The concern led to a focus on defining the capital and the adequacy levels that financial institutions must observe for their own safety and also in the wider interest of society. In the fast-changing world of finance, a regular watch was needed to make the concept work while maintaining economic dynamism. The Basel Committee on Banking Supervision (BCBS), an organ of the Bank for International Settlements, keeps that watch and, to that end, it has developed the concept of capital adequacy for banks.

The Committee defines the capital adequacy norms for the institutions individually. Each company has to fulfill the requirements that the Committee defines for it, with reference to the four categories of capital, which are called the 'tiers'. Since 1988, the BCSB has issued three Accords on capital adequacy standards that banks across the globe have to adhere to. These Accords also have implications for Islamic financial services and remain under review by scholars, regulators, and supervisors alike. Let us briefly explain each of these Accords. We shall begin with an explanation of the concepts of capital, its classes (tiers), risk weights, and the calculation of the adequacy ratios as a backdrop for the main discussion on the Accords. The reason is that what is discussed in the following section is common to all Accords.

10.3.3.2 On- and off-balance-sheet items

The assets (and liabilities) of banks and other financial institutions are recorded in their balance sheets. The distinction is not exclusive. At times, on-balance-sheet assets may become off-balance-sheet assets and vice versa; it all depends on managerial decisions. How, then, do we explain the term 'off-balance-sheet assets' and how are such assets different from 'on-balance-sheet assets'? The essential difference is that on-balance-sheet assets form part of the asset side total of the balance sheet, whereas off-balance-sheet assets remain outside this total. However, this need not convey that off-balance-sheet assets are not shown on the balance sheet; they are recorded there. Let us illustrate. Broadly, the following situations give rise to off-balance-sheet assets:

a   Debts that the bank advances to clients are included in its on-balance-sheet assets, but if the same debts are securitized and sold to third parties, they cease to be the assets of the bank. However, the bank may still manage the securities thus created for its customers. They become off -balance-sheet assets for the bank but are recorded in the form of a note in the balance sheet. It may be mentioned here that as Islam does not allow the securitization of debts, they remain off the balance sheet except in Malaysia, where *bay'al-dayn* (sale of debt) is allowed.
b   Money deposited by clients in their regular accounts creates corresponding liabilities for the banks. However, if some clients choose to transfer their deposits to a money market mutual fund, the corresponding liability of the bank would end, although the bank may continue to manage the amount transferred to the fund. If the funds were used to purchase, say, shares or units, they would constitute off-balance-sheet assets for the bank.

Thus, a bank itself has no direct claim to the assets we have just mentioned, although it usually has some basic fiduciary responsibilities to meet for the clients. Banks may report off-balance-sheet items in their accounting statements formally. They can also refer to "assets under management", a figure that is included in the on- and off-balance-sheet items.

10.3.3.3 Risk-weighted approach

Different classes of assets have different degrees of risk associated with them, determining their quality status. Thus, for calculating the capital adequacy ratio (CAR) we have to take the risk-weighted aggregate of the assets. The risk-weighted approach is preferable for the following reasons: (a) It provides an easier way of comparing banks across different jurisdictions. (b) Off-balance-sheet exposures can be easily included in capital adequacy estimates. (c) Banks are free to carry low-risk liquid assets in their accounts books.

To illustrate, assets, such as debentures (corporate bonds for long-term financing), are assigned a higher risk than other assets, such as cash or over government securities. Since different types of assets have different levels of risk, weighing assets based on their risk profiles adjusts for assets that are less risky by allowing banks to discount such assets. The most basic application may allow government debt even a 0% risk weighting, that is, they are subtracted from total assets for the purpose of calculating the CAR. The formula for calculating the ratio is simple:

$$CAR = \frac{Tier1 capital + Tier2 capital}{Aggregate risk\ weighted assets}, \tag{10.1}$$

Where Tier 1 capital = Total equity − Revaluation reserves Tier 2 capital = Revaluation reserves + subordinated debt + Hybrid capital + Provisions including Deferred tax + Total loan loss and other reserves. In light of the previous groundwork, you may find it easier to follow the discussion on the Basel Accords that follows.

10.4 Basel Accords

10.4.1 Basel I (1988)

The first Basel Accord was simple and straightforward as it was essentially an agreement negotiated between the Basel Committee member countries and was initially applicable only to those whose banks were operating at the international level. The Accord received prompt acceptance not only from the Basel country banks but also from other global institutions. Basel I divided the capital of banks into two tiers on the basis of differences in the quality of their assets, as already discussed earlier in the chapter. Each of the two tiers was assigned a 4% risk weight that considered only credit risk, leaving out others, thus making the overall CAR equal to 8%. As this ratio was intended to define the minimum, not the optimal capital requirement level for a bank, it was assumed that the well-capitalized banks would go in for higher ratios in order to cover the market and operational risks the Accord had left out.

One often-mentioned aspect of Basel I is the so-called three pillars on which it rests. The first pillar is made up of the minimum capital requirements. It seeks closer proximity between bank capital and its risk exposures. The second pillar focuses on supervisory review, as the supervisor has to promote the overall safety of the banking system, even though individual banks are not outside its ambit. And the third pillar aims at enforcing market discipline through its involvement in the capital adequacy regimen. The three pillars are intended to work in unison toward achieving specified goals.

10.4.2 Basel II (2004)

The limitations of the Basel I Accord surfaced over the years and led the Basel Committee to revise the standards of capital adequacy for internationally active banks. The Basel II Accord was published in June 2004 and was titled *International Convergence of Capital Measurement and Capital Standards: A Revised Framework*. The framework was further amended in July 2005. We cannot discuss the framework details here, as these are mostly technical rather than conceptual. However, a few provisions can be highlighted.

One relates to the assigning of risk weights for the profit-sharing assets. This would have wide ramifications for Islamic finance, especially for its *mudarabah* and *musharakah* models, as they generate assets that are either profit-and-loss sharing or profit-and-risk-sharing. Both have commodities or other assets held for trading. Such assets are difficult to ascribe to the market risk concept of Basel I and have attracted the attention of the IFSB when it set its version of the Capital Adequacy Standard for IFIs. Credit risk is no problem in their case but another type of risk – displaced commercial risk – does become an issue. We have postponed our discussion of this topic until this chapter, but let us deal with it now.

10.4.2.1 Displaced commercial risk

Islamic banks differ from conventional banks in a significant way: they mobilize funds in the form of profit-sharing investment deposits. In theory, depositors earn the returns on their money from the net earnings of the assets their funds finance in a pre-agreed ratio, but *all* losses fall on the assets financed in this way – i.e., on deposits except in the case of misconduct, negligence, or any breach of the contract terms by the Islamic bank. However, in practice, all losses do not fall on investment deposit holders. Under commercial or regulatory pressure, the majority of Islamic banks are obliged to absorb a proportion of losses normally borne by the depositors. If they did not do so, they would run the risk of a massive withdrawal of funds from the bank. This practice exposes Islamic banks to a unique risk, called the 'displaced commercial risk', which requires allocating adequate

138 Law regulation and governance

capital to ensure smooth returns on profit-sharing investment deposits and/ or to cover losses. The factor contributes to an increase in the CAR for Islamic banks. The measurement of the actual risk of profit sharing would depend on the returns-smoothing policies of the Islamic bank.

10.4.3 Basel III (2010–2011)

Building on and carrying forward the Basel II framework, the BCBS published its third Accord, popularly known as Basel III, in 2010–2011. It was intended to be introduced over the period beginning from 1 April 2013 until 31 March 2018. *The Basel III Report*, published in book form, is a comprehensive document focusing on the consistency of risk weightings for banking assets generated by a mechanism developed under Basel II. The salient features of the Accord are briefly as follows:

- **Capital requirements**: In addition to raising the capital requirement ratios for both tiers, Basel III introduces two more capital buffers: (i) a 2.5% capital conservation obligatory buffer, and (ii) a counter-cyclical buffer, which would allow national regulators to require up to another 2.5% of capital during periods of high credit growth. The adoption of this proposal is not compulsory.
- **Leverage ratio**: Basel III introduces a minimum *leverage ratio* that is calculated by dividing Tier 1 capital by the bank's average total assets. The banks are expected to maintain a leverage ratio in excess of 3%. In July 2013, the US Federal Reserve Bank announced that the minimum leverage ratio would be 6% for eight systemically important financial institutions and 5% for their bank holding companies. A systemically important financial institution is a bank (insurance company or other financial institution) whose failure might trigger a financial crisis.
- **Liquidity requirements**: Basel III used two obligatory liquidity ratios. One is the *liquidity coverage ratio*, which requires a bank to hold sufficient high-quality liquid assets to cover its total net cash outflows over 30 days. The other is the *net stable funding ratio*, which requires the available amount of stable funding to exceed the amount needed to cover a one-year period of extended stress, i.e. the exposure of bank capital levels to turbulent economic and financial scenarios.

Thus, Basel III tightens the leverage ratio framework and disclosure requirements for banks and other financial institutions to enforce discipline in the wavering financial markets. Critics say that the step will slow down growth rates but bumpy rides may also eventually result in lower rates. In Europe, regulators are insistent on implementing the Basel Accords. Smaller banks may have some breathing space in the suffocating competition. Islamic financiers may find the provisions of Basel III supportive of their ethical temperament.

10.4.4 Basel Accords and Islamic finance

Islamic finance operates as an integral part of the global financial system. As such, Islamic banks have to fall in line with international regulations as and when enforced. This adds to the unidirectional convergence of the systems discussed earlier, in Chapter 4. The Basel Committee Accords on capital adequacy measures have forced the pace of such convergence. Basel I was narrowly focused on the banks of the Committee member countries and was of little consequence for Islamic banks. Basel III recommendations are in the process of being implemented over time. Thus, it is Basel II standards that demand consideration in the present context. These standards have a blanket reach, covering banks across the globe. Islamic bankers and jurists found some of the prescriptions of the Accord incompatible with the nature of Islamic banks' portfolios. For instance, the equity estimation for Islamic banks must include not only the bank owners' stakes but also the investment deposits involved in participatory contracts.

Since the aim of these Accords is to have an adequate level of capital available in the bank for risk management, the following discussion is contextual to the risk weighting of assets. It is also important to mention that in the calculation of risk weights, banks have the choice of adopting the Basel II framework for the calculation of capital adequacy or the internally set standards, with its approval. The choice has allowed the central banks of countries to modify standards to accommodate their domestic requirements. For example, in 2007 the Reserve Bank of New Zealand simplified its explanation and examples of capital adequacy ratios and calculated the same for local banks.

Various sorts of standards for the IFIs are set by the two autonomous international institutions – the AAOIFI and the IFSB. The AAOIFI sets the *Shari'ah*-compliance standards for entering the Islamic financial markets. The objective is to build the confidence of the populace in Islamic finance by ensuring, in addition, the transparency of the transaction and protection of the depositors' interests. Introduced in 2001, the new one covers the following areas:

- The Standardized Approach to Credit Risk
- The Internal Ratings-Based Approach to Credit Risk
- Asset Securitization • Operational Risk
- Pillar 2: Supervisory Review Process
- Management and Supervision of Interest Rate Risk in the Banking Book
- Pillar 3: Market Discipline

10.5 Islam and governance

Corporate governance became a prominent issue following the 2002 introduction of the reformatory Sarbanes–Oxley Act in the USA, which was intended to elevate the sagging confidence in financing companies and markets because of rising accounting fraud that bankrupted many high-profile companies, including, for example, Enron and World.com. Efficient and honest corporate governance has since become a pressing issue in the development of a vibrant and sound finance industry – conventional or Islamic.

The governance of financial institutions is a vast and complicated subject. It rose to prominence following the 2007 financial turmoil ground to dust the mighty banks, the giant insurance companies, and funds overnight. From that dust rose the concern for honesty, transparency, and efficiency in corporate management; the more exalted term being governance.

Arguably, the regulation of Islamic finance needs to be aligned with the regulation of conventional finance to the maximum extent consistent with *Shari'ah* requirements because the two systems compete in common markets. This would enable the believers to participate fully (with all the advantages) in mainstream international finance and capital markets. This means applying the internationally accepted standards and principles to Islamic finance with the modifications needed to make them *Shari'ah*-compliant. Even so, there are still other ingredients for completing the Islamic financial framework.

10.5.1 Definition and scope

Corporate governance has to be firmly geared to the vision of the organization. It must fix its targets to that end and promote an administrative work culture appropriate for achieving those targets. This requires framing rules, practices, and processes that can help direct the company and ensure there are built-in controls that keep it on the right course. In addition, governance involves designing checks and balances to harmonize the conflicting interests of the various stakeholders in the company – i.e., its shareholders, managers, workers, suppliers, financiers, customers, public authorities, and the community at large. Corporate governance thus encompasses virtually every sphere of management, including action plans, the implementation of those plans, and monitoring to ensure its goals are achieved.

We cannot cover the numerous topics falling in this ambit here, so we will limit the discussion to the two significant aspects of Islamic finance relating to governance: (i) the structural layers and (ii) participatory finance. We begin with the structure of governance, which is in a continual state of evolution, and follow that with a discussion on participatory finance, where the focal point will be the sharing of profit and the bearing of losses in the system. You will recall that we have discussed the latter in earlier chapters, so we shall re-examine it here briefly in the context of governance.

10.5.2 Shari'ah governance

There is frequent mention of *Shari'ah* governance in the literature on Islamic finance but the notion remains rather indeterminate due to the rapid growth of the industry, juristic diversities, divergent standards, and multiplicity of authorities. Even the following definition of the term that the IFSB attempted to provide is reflective of its being in a state of flux

However, under the circumstances, this is a good generic definition. As most banks adopt a corporate form of business organization, governance in Islamic finance requires the IFIs scrupulously adjust corporate norms, rules, and procedures to *Shari'ah* requirements in form and substance. Note that the present governance structure of IFIs has three layers: notional regional and international. As Islamic finance is part of the overall global markets, its structures bear the notable imprints of the legal, regulatory and supervisory provisions at the international level, especially from the Organisation for Economic Co-operation and Development (OECD) and the three Basel Accords, as discussed earlier. The OECD principles include

I.   ensuring the basis for an effective corporate governance framework;
II.   spelling out the rights of shareholders and key ownership functions;
III. ensuring an equitable treatment of shareholders;
IV.   determining the role of stakeholders in corporate governance;
V.   seeking disclosure and transparency; and
VI.   specifying the responsibilities of the Board of Governance.

National-level governance framework: This consists of banking sector-specific laws, codes and guidelines, stock exchanges' listings, rules and regulations, listed companies, regulatory authorities, laws, rules, and regulations.

Regional-level Shari'ah-**specific standards**: These include IFSB Guiding Principles on *Shari'ah* Governance systems for institutions offering Islamic financial services 2009; IFSB Guiding Principles on Corporate Governance for institutions offering only Islamic financial services 2006; IFSB guidance on key elements in the supervisory review process of institutions offering Islamic financial services 2007; AAOIFI Accounting, Auditing and Governance Standards for IFIs. These provisions do not cover Islamic insurance (*takaful*) institutions and Islamic mutual funds. We have discussed these items on a selective basis in earlier chapters

10.5.2.1 Participatory finance

The differences between theory and practice are as apparent in Islamic financial governance at the institutional level as they are in the theory and practice of participatory finance, the distinctive feature of the Islamic system. The two sets of differences seem to feed on one another. Participatory finance – primarily *mudarabah* – is a risk- and reward-sharing mode of financing. We have discussed elsewhere the theory as to how this is accomplished and who gets what. However, what is most important for corporate governance is to determine how to resolve the inevitable and perennial conflicts of interest that sharing causes between different stakeholders in the IFIs. Conventional finance is also not free from conflicts of interest,

142 Law regulation and governance

but these are of a different sort. Take, for instance, the conflict of interest between the shareholders of a bank and its depositors. In conventional banks, the issue is how much interest to pay to savings account holders.

But this does not need any negotiations between the parties because the interest rate is determined by the market. In contrast, conflict over the sharing of profit going to investment depositors is an entirely different matter. The profit share paid to them will depend on what is deemed to be a fair division of profits between the parties. The division ratios are not determined, unlike interest rates, by external forces but are settled *within* the Islamic financial institution. The trade-off between the interests aims at 'paying a competitive return to depositors while maintaining a dividend to shareholders which is sufficient to ensure that they continue to hold their investment rather than selling the shares' (Rodney). To strike a trade-off that is equally satisfactory to the parties is a ticklish issue for the Board of Governors. Depositors, being the outsiders *vis-à-vis* the shareholders, invariably have perceptions of adverse discrimination. This has the potential of giving rise to bank–client court cases. There is a strong case for depositors to be represented on the Board to mitigate such possibilities.

10.6 Summary points

- Islamic finance is the fastest-growing segment of the global finance industry. IFIs operate today in 75 countries worldwide. Lack of uniformity in products and standards hinders the progress of Islamic finance. However, efforts to improve uniformity through various institutions and organizations are being made to close cross-country gaps and the results are positive. Nevertheless, divergence in principles and practices within limits has advantages as well.
- Despite its rapid growth, Islamic finance has been confined to the rich of society and has yet to touch the ordinary citizen. The societal utility of the system is expected to improve with the passage of time, and shifts in public policies are intended to improve the lot of the weaker sections of society.
- instruments a mirror image of the latter. Concern has been voiced at times about the merging of Islamic finances into the mainstream, where it loses its purpose and direction. This chapter has looked at Islamic finance with reference to three important aspects: law, regulation, and governance. The coverage is vast, so we have deliberately kept the discussion brief, but simple and clear.
- The Islamic financial system is heavily influenced by common law, which is based on custom and heritage, and civil law, which is the result of legislative activity. Both the common law and civil law have pre-Islamic origins but regained dominance due to the long rule of the colonial powers over the Muslim world.

- After achieving independence, Muslim countries could naturally not change gear abruptly. However, Islamic law is slowly but surely making its presence felt in the sphere of finance, supported by a favorable constellation of forces.
- Operating parallel to and in competition with conventional banks limits the policy options of the IFIs. They are constrained by the observance of international norms and rules, and IFIs have been slow to implement the Islamic requirements and changes that are needed.
- The issue of allowing Islamic windows in conventional banks, which was once a controversial matter, is now a dead issue. Attempts to close windows were not successful at the international level for a variety of reasons, but especially because it was not difficult to circumvent the law, and banks found it easy to defeat the objective of their abolition.
- The rise in the severity, frequency, duration, and contagion of financial crises after the 1880s, culminating with the worst crisis of 2007, led to a major reversal in global economic thought and policy concerning the behavior of the financial system across countries. The slogan of globalization, liberalization, and privatization has given way almost overnight to demands for intervention, regulation, supervision, and tight governance of financial institutions, especially those having a global presence.
- Regulatory bodies at the national, regional, and international levels have now sprung up, and their activities are being coordinated. Banks and other financial institutions at their own level are tightening administration, the OECD has announced regulatory principles, and the Basel Committee Accords all point to the intention that the end of unbridled freedom for financial institutions and markets is in sight.

Appendix

Islamic finance
Brief history

Egypt was one of the first countries to adopt Islamic banking, but its development there has been very uneven because of the changing character of the successive political structures of the country. The first Islamic bank was launched by Ahmad El Najjar under a secular cover for fear of being seen as a symbol of the Islamic revivalism that was distasteful to the political establishment of the country. The bank took the form of a savings bank that was based on profit sharing in the Nile Delta town of Mit Ghamr in 1963. That particular experiment was short-lived – the bank had to close in 1967 – but soon there were nine such banks operating in Egypt. These banks worked without taking or giving interest. They invested mostly in trade and industry, directly or in partnership with others on a profit-sharing basis. They worked as saving-investment units, not as commercial banks. Anwar Sadat, the then president of Egypt, established the first public sector bank in 1971. The Nasir Social Bank operated as an interest-free institution, although it did not declare any commitment to Islamic law. In the 1980s, a number of Islamic banks collapsed under trying conditions and the savings of many Egyptians were completely lost. The recent pro-democracy revolution in the country raises expectations that Islamic finance may get a boost. The global acceptance and expansion of Islamic finance strengthen this expectation.

Banking in **Iran** was rationalized on the heels of the Islamic revolution in 1979.

The 35 banking units working in the country were merged into 6 commercial and 3 specialized banks. A law for interest-free banking was passed in 1983, and banks were asked to discard interest payments by 21 March 1984. All banking transactions were to follow Islamic law. They were allowed to take in two types of deposits. First, *qard hasan*, which covered current and savings accounts. Such deposits are treated as the bank's resources, and any return on them is decided by the bank's management. The second are investment deposits, the return on which accrues according to a profit-sharing contract. Banking products are based on Islamic contracts – musharakah, mudarabah, ijara installment transactions; direct investment; forward transactions; and so on – which are all allowed and will be explained in the chapters, but markup activities are most popular in Iran. Lending on a fixed rate of return is permitted because fixing the rate does not necessarily equate to charging/paying interest in the Shiite law. The use of interest is allowable in foreign exchange transactions. Iran has the potential of emerging as the single largest market in Islamic finance. Six Iranian banks appear among the top ten Islamic financial institutions worldwide. Iran presently accounts for more than a third of *Shari'ah*-compliant global assets, exceeding that of any other country.

Malaysia leads the world today in Islamic finance practice. The first Islamic finance institution in the country emerged with the innovative idea of enabling Muslims of small means to save enough money over time to perform the *Hajj* pilgrimage to Mecca. This culminated in the establishment of the Muslim Pilgrims' Savings Corporation in 1963. Gradually, the institution evolved into the Pilgrims Management and Fund Board, or *Tabung Haji*, as it is now known. The institution accepts deposits in installments from those intending to go for the pilgrimage. It invests the savings so collected as per Shari'ah norms. However, its role as a financier is rather limited; it is a non-bank institution. The success of *Tabung Haji* revealed the potential and possibilities for Islamic finance in the country. It inspired the establishment of *Bank Islam Malaysia* in 1983 as the first full-scale Islamic commercial bank of Malaysia, the *Tabung* contributing RM10 million to its initial equity of RM80 million. The bank has since expanded quickly and now has 122 branches spread all over the country, with paid-up capital touching the RM180 million mark. May bank Islamic Ber had today is ranked first in Malaysia and with assets over $100 billion, the Bloomberg survey (2013) finds it the 13th strongest bank worldwide in the overall rankings.

In 1993, commercial banks, merchant banks, and finance companies were allowed to offer Islamic banking products and services under the Islamic Banking Scheme. They were, however, required to separate the funds and activities of Islamic banking transactions from those of the conventional banking business to avoid any mingling of funds with mainstream business. Mainstream commercial banks could also operate 'Islamic windows' (i.e., Islamic counters in conventional banks) by observing similar conditions. However, this facility was later withdrawn, and commercial banks interested in running Islamic businesses now have to open exclusive branches for this purpose.

The Dow Jones of New York and RHB Securities of Kuala Lumpur have jointly launched a new 'Islamic Malaysia Index', which is based on a sample of Malaysian companies' stocks that comply with the specified *Shari'ah* norms. For example, these norms require that for inclusion in the index, the total debt of a company – its total cash plus interest-bearing securities and its accounts receivables – must each be less than 33% of the trailing 12-month average capitalization. Bank Negara Malaysia – the central bank of the country – has made untiring efforts, under its governor Zeti, to promote Islamic finance at home and abroad on various fronts – the development of products, the design of regulatory standards, juridical research, Islamic finance education, and training – through INCEIF, the Global University of Islamic Finance, which it established in 2004.

Pakistan's contribution to Islamic banking was evaluated by a committee of religious leaders and scholars of undivided India. They were of the opinion that Islamic banking in the country could not rise enough to meet popular expectations in range or depth. Political uncertainty, foreign dominance, a series of wars, and, finally, the separation of East Pakistan, now Bangladesh, did not provide much space for the expansion of Islamic finance until 1977, when the Islamic lobby, growing in strength and influence, was able to extract important concessions and support from the military government of President Zia-ul-Haq. A comprehensive program of Islamization in various sectors – economic, social, and political – was launched. The International Islamic University was established in Islamabad in 1983 and the Second International Conference on Islamic Economics was held there the same year. A process of economic Islamization was simultaneously initiated with a time frame of three years.

Consequently, all the commercial banking operations were made 'interest-free' from 1 July 1985. Recently, the State Bank of Pakistan has allowed the formation of full-fledged Islamic banks in the private sector. The existing scheduled commercial banks can also open subsidiaries for running Islamic finance operations. The State Bank of Pakistan has laid down detailed criteria for setting up such subsidiaries, including the proviso that a minimum of 49% of the shares shall be offered for public subscription. An interesting feature of interest-free finance in Pakistan has been the growing popularity of *mudarabah* companies which operate essentially on the supply side of the market – they accept deposits from the public to invest in businesses on a profit-sharing basis. Of about half a dozen Islamic banks operating in Pakistan, *Meezan*, with 54 branches spread all over the country, is leading the pack. The popularity of Islamic banking is on the rise in Pakistan in recent years, with deposits going up from about US$3 billion to US$4 billion in 2011. This can partly be attributed to the large-scale failure of banks during the global financial turmoil since 2007 and partly to a surge in the perception among the dominantly Muslim society that their faith is under attack from the West. Nevertheless, Islamic banks operate on the fringes of the banking system and their share of the market has barely crossed the 8% mark.

Middle East and North Africa (the **MENA** region) have emerged as important areas in the development of Islamic banking. The constituent countries dominate their financial services including the following:

The investment and mutual funds project finance companies and *takaful* institutions. The characteristic feature of Islamic finance here is its industry-led approach to development instead of the regulatory approach adopted elsewhere. As a result, global players have been attracted to the region despite concerns about the lack of a focused and cohesive regulatory framework.

The area is vast, extending from Morocco to Iran and to Yemen in the south, and comprises numerous countries – big and small – whose interpretations of the religious injunctions vary. In many countries, with the exception of the United Arab Emirates and Bahrain, Islamic banks are regulated and supervised mostly in the same way as conventional banks. The business-led attitude of the region today accounts for 75% of *Shari'ah*-compliant assets worldwide, although initially, Southeast Asia led the development of Islamic finance.

India is a secular socialist democracy and does not, in principle, encourage public recognition or support of institutions with sectarian denominations. As such, there is no Islamic bank working in India at present under the legal framework of the country. But individuals are free to initiate and promote religion-based activities for the general benefit under Indian legislation. Thus, Islamic finance institutions (not banks) proliferated in India in the private sector in contrast to Muslim countries, where Islamic finance is essentially in the public domain. India has the second-largest Muslim population in the world. Initially, Muslims were the poorest and most socially isolated members of the community, who were left behind by the creation of Pakistan, and they now comprise a 10%–12% minority of the Indian population. Survival instinct, the necessity to compete in order to get along, and deepening democracy gave them the strength to rise from being regarded almost as the lowest of the low to being able to hold their own in the socioeconomic environment of the country. Today, Muslims are valued for their honesty, commitment, hard work, and technical acumen in small and medium-sized businesses. The rising tide of liberalization and privatization has opened doors for employment opportunities as the market acknowledges merit more than public enterprise. The Muslim community has also earned its share in rising prosperity abroad.

Presently, they own and manage innumerable artisan-based production units in prosperous parts of the country. Muslim Indians are not devoid of religious aspirations and want to lead a life conforming to Islamic norms. It is reported that in 1990–1991, of the total commercial bank loans granted in India, the share of Muslim borrowings was no more than 5%. Even if one acknowledges the existence of discrimination, as some argue, a possible reason to explain this percentage being much lower than the proportion of the Muslim population in the urban centers of the country may simply be because Muslims avoid borrowing on interest.

Supportive of this hypothesis is the fact that even though none of the acts regulating financial institutions in India admits the possibility of launching an interest-free bank, Muslim Indians have made constant efforts to explore the possibilities of establishing interest-free financial institutions within the existing legal framework. At present, more than 200 such institutions are operating in India. No reliable statistics are available on their performance, nor is there any scientific information system for making queries about them. Most of them are established by individuals connected with one or the other Islamic movement. Most of them are registered under the general Societies Act of India and can be broadly classified as Interest-free Credit Associations, Interest-free Financial Companies, or Investment Funds. In 1992, Rehmatullah published a research paper on the subject, which provides some useful information on what he misnames 'Islamic banks' in India.

Bibliography

Al-Amine, M.B.M. (2008). Sukuk market: innovations and challenges. *Islamic Economic Studies*, Vol. 15, No. 2, pp. 1–22.

Al-Maghrabi, N.B.M. (2013). Conceptual analysis of Islamic home financing models. *ISRA Journal of Islamic Finance*, Vol. 5, pp. 29–88.

Al-Sadr, M.B. (1984). *Iqtisaduna (Our Economics)*, 1st edition, Volume 2, English translation. Tehran, Iran: World Organization for Islamic Services.

Askari, H., Iqbal, Z., Krichene, N., & Mirakhor, A. (2012). *Risk Sharing in Finance: The Islamic Finance Alternative*. Singapore: Wiley.

Bhatti, M., & Bhatti, I. (2009). Development in legal Issues of corporate governance in Islamic Finance. *Journal of Economic & Administrative Sciences*, Vol. 25, No. 1, pp. 67–91.

Cecilia, T. (2005). Sustainable development: A critical assessment of past and present views. In *Appraising Sustainable Development: Water Management and Environmental Challenges*, edited by Asit K. Biswas and Cecilia Tortajada. New Delhi: Oxford University Press, pp. 1–17.

Chambers, M.S., Garage, C., & Sehlagehauf, D. (2007). *Mortgage Contracts and Housing Tenure Decisions*, Working Paper, Federal Reserve Bank of St. Louis (Research Division), pp. 1–40.

Craig, N. (2012). *Islamic Finance: Law and Practice*. United Kingdom: David Eisenberg Google Books.

El-Gamal, M. (2014). *Exploitative Profit Sharing: On the Incoherence of All Contract-Based Approaches to "Islamic Finance."* Accessed on 21 April 2014.

El-Gamal, M.A. (2006). *Islamic Finance: Law, Economics and Practice*. Cambridge, NY: Cambridge University Press.

Exald, F. (2020). *Insurance and Risk*. Springer Nature Switzerland AG. http://lchc.ucsd.edu/cogn_150/Readings/ewald/ewald.pdf

Halim, A. (2001). *The Deferred Contracts of Exchange: Al-Qur'an in Contrast with the Islamic Economists' Theory on Banking and Finance*. Kuala Lumpur, Malaysia: IKIM.

Hamza, H., & Jedidia, K.B. (2017). Money: Time value and time preference in Islamic perspective. *Turkish Journal of Islamic Economics*, Vol. 4, No. 2, pp. 19–35.

Hanohan, P. (2001). *Islamic Financial Intermediation: Economic and Prudential Considerations*. The World Bank. WB

Hasan, M., & Dridi, J. (2010). *The Effects of Global Crisis on Islamic and Conventional Banks: A Comparative Study*, IMF Working Paper 10/201.

150 Bibliography

Hasan, Z. (2002). Mudarabah as a mode of financing in Islamic banking: Theory, and practice middle east business and economic review, Vol. 14, No. 2, Sydney, Australia, pp. 41–53

Hasan, Z. (2008a). Credit creation and control: An unresolved issue in Islamic banking. *JKAU*, Vol. 52, No. 2, pp. 69–81.

Hasan, Z. (2008b). Risk-sharing: The sole basis of Islamic finance? *Time for a Serious Rethink JKAU: Islamic Economics Institute*, Vol. 29, No. 2, pp. 23–36.

Hasan, Z. (2010). Islamic finance – The structure objective mismatch ISRA. *International Journal of Islamic Finance*, Vol. 2, No. 1. pp. 7–21.

Hasan, Z. (2011). Islamic home finance in the social mirror. *ISRA International Journal of Islamic Finance*, Vol. 3, No.1, pp. 7–24.

Hasan, Z. (2013). A critique of the diminishing balance method of Islamic home financing response. *ISRA International Journal of Islamic Finance*, Vol. 5, No. 1, pp. 7–23.

Hasan, Z. (2014). Basel accords financial turmoil and Islamic banking. *ISRA International Journal of Islamic Finance*, Vol. 6, No. 1, pp. 21–48.

Hasan, Z. (2015a). *Islamic Banking and Finance – An Integrative Approach*. Kuala Lumpur, Malaysia: Oxford University Press.

Hasan, Z. (2015b). Risk sharing versus risk transfer in Islamic finance: A critical appraisal. *ISRA International Journal of Islamic Finance*, Vol. 7, No. 1, pp. 7–24.

Hasan, Z. (2016). PLS finance and monetary policy: An new measure mooted. *Journal of Reviews on Global Economics*, Vol. 5, pp. 288–297.

Hasan, Z. (2021). Risk sharing versus risk transfer in Islamic finance – A critical appraisal, Chap. 8. In *Some Controversial Topics in Islamic Economics and Finance*. Jeddah: Scientific Publishing Centre, KAU.

Howladar, K. (2010). Shariah risk: Understanding recent compliance issues in Islamic finance. Moody's Investor Service Report.

Hussain, A. (2010). *Islamic Home Financing and Mortgages*. Islamic Mortgages. co.uk. Accessed on 1 January 2012.

Ijaz, M. (2017). *Islamic Modes of Financing*. Pakistan: AL-ADWA37:27 Islamic.

Ilias, S. (2010). Islamic finance: Overview and policy concerns. Congressional Research Service. *International Journal of Law and Management*, Vol. 53, No. 1, pp. 51–61.

Karl, B. (1964). The economic theory of insurance (Notes for an informal discussion in Edinburgh). https://www.casact.org/sites/default/files/database/astin_vol4no3_252.pdf

Kettell, B. (2011). *Introduction to Islamic Banking and Finance*. Hoboken, NJ: John Wiley.

Knight, F.H. (1921). *Risk, Uncertainty and Profit*. Boston: Houghton Mifflin.

Laldin, M.A. (2013). *Islamic Legal Maxims & Their Applications in Islamic Finance*.Malaysia: ISRA.

Malim Nurhafizah, A.K. (2015). Bank margins in OIC countries: Islamic and conventional banks compared (Unpublished PhD dissertation).

Md Husin, M., & Haron, R. (2020). Takāful demand: A review of selected literature. *ISRA International Journal of Islamic Finance*, Vol. 12, No. 3, pp. 443–455. doi: 10.1108/IJIF-03-2019-0046

Meera, A.K.M. (2012). A critique of diminishing balance method of Islamic home financing. *ISRA International Journal of Islamic Finance*, Vol. 4, No. 2, pp. 7–23.

Meera, A.K.M., & Razak, D.A. (2009). Home financing through the Musharakah Mutanaqisah contracts: some practical issues. *JKAU: Islamic Economics*, Vol. 22, No.1, pp. 3–25.

Muhammad, I. (2017). AL-ADWA37:27, Pakistan.

Rosley, S.A. (2008). *Critical Issues on Islamic Banking and Financial Markets*. Kuala Lumpur, Malaysia: Dinamas Publishing.

Securities Commission Malaysia. (2009). *Introduction to Islamic Capital Market*. Petaling Jaya, Malaysia: Lexis Nexis.

Syed Ali, S., & Ahmad, A. (Eds.). (2007). *Islamic Banking and Finance – Fundamentals and Contemporary Issues*. Jeddah: Islamic Development Bank.

Usmani, M.T. (2009). Sukuk and their contemporary applications. http://www.iefpedia.com/english/wp-content/uploads/2009/11/Sukuk-and-their-Contemporary-Applications.pdf. Accessed on 1 September 2021.

Wilson, R. (2012). *Legal, Regulatory and Governance Issues in Islamic Finance*. United Kingdom: Edinburgh University Press.

Index

Pages in *italics* refer figures and pages in **bold** refer tables.

Abbas 37
Abu Dhabi Islamic Bank (ADIB) 84
Accounting and Auditing Organization
for Islamic Financial Institutions
(AAOIFI) 103, 131; guidance
80–81; Standard No. 8 64; Standard
No. 17 77; Standard No. 25 70;
Standards 62, 81–82, 139
African Development Bank 128
Ahmad, Imam 66
Al-aada al-muhakkamah 38
Al-Dararyuzalu 37
Alexandria 28
Alhamdolillah 44
al kharaj bi al daman 65
Al-mashaqqahtajibu al-tasir 37–38
Al-Umur-bi-masidha 37
Al-Yaqin la yazulu bi-al shakk 37
awqaf 83

Bahrain 52, 78, 80, 85, 131, 147
bai-al-inah 83, 87
Basel Accords: Basel I (1988) 136–137;
Basel II (2004) 137–138; Basel
III (2010–2011) 138; and Islamic
finance 139
The Basel Committee on Banking
Supervision (BCBS) 134, 138
The Bay Bitehamam Ajil (BBA) 58;
structure 70–71, *71*; variants 52–53
BSC 81
business cycles 20, 24
business risk 94, 97, 101; *see also* Islam
and financial risks

Cairo 28
capital adequacy ratio (CAR) 136

capitalism 93, 107
capital markets 61, *61*
central banking 3, 10, 30
central bank of India 50
central bank of Iran 25, 27
Chapra, M. U. 33
CIMB 84, 87
Clark, J. B. 26
coinage of gold dinar 33–34
conventional banks 8, 32, 36, 39, 41,
49, 57, 65, 99–100, 127–128, 137,
142–143, 145, 147
conventional bond 75–77, 89
conventional finance 18, 31, 35, 103,
108, 112, 126, 140–141
conventional insurance 109, 114–116,
120, 122–123
Cooperative and Mutual Fund
Insurance Federation 120
corporate equity capital 95
corporate governance 139–140
credit 1; control 14; creation 2, 13–14,
14; volume of 2
credit risk (CR) 98, *100*
currency risk 100–101, 103–105

depression 7, 12–13
displaced commercial risk (DCR) *100*,
101
Dubai Islamic Bank (DIB), 2005 81

Egypt 144
El Najjar, Ahmad 144
enterprise risk management (ERM)
framework: derivatives and risk
mitigation 102–103; exchange risk
hedging 103–105; financial swaps

Index 153

105–106, **106**; firm proactive 101; options 105; risk management process 102, *102*; societal well-being 102

entrepreneurs 12–13, 15, 18, 39–40, 79, 82, 92–93, 98, 107, 119

equal monthly installments (EMIs) 48–52; compounding element in **52**; home financing *51*

equity investment risk (EIR) *100*, 101

ethical funds 29

Ex post profit 95

fiduciary risk (FR) 98, *100*

finance 9; and money 1–2; and wealth creation 2–3

financial instruments: hire purchase and rent sharing 67; and interbank investment 60; *Istisna* 69, *69*; leasing/*ijarah* 66–67; *Murabahah* 42; *Musharakah* 43; *salam* 67–68

financial markets 59; capital 61; direct and indirect modes *61*, 61–62; money 60–61

financial risks: adversity 91; *ex ante* concept 95; explorations 91–92; profit and 92–93

Financial Services and Markets Act 2000 131

Financial Services Authority (FSA) 131–132

financing modes 70; BBA structure 70–71, *71*; indirect instruments 73; *tawarruq* in Islamic finance 71–72, *72*

The Fire Office 111

foreign exchange (FX) 104; risk 100–101

Franklin, Benjamin 111

General Theory of Employment, Interest and Money 6

gross domestic product (GDP) 24, 49

The Gulf Cooperation Council (GCC) 88

Gulf International Bank 81

Hamad Medical City (HMC) in Doha 78

homeownership 46

HSBC 81

ijara 43, 59, 66–67, 90; *sukuk* 82–83, *83*

ijarah-mawsufahfi-al dhimmah 87

inah 52, 71, 88, 90, 130, 133

INCEIF 47, 130, 146

India 22, 25, 27, 146–148

Indian firm 101, 104

Indian National Stock Exchange 104

inflation/deflation 7, 12, 20

installment payment 21, 31, 42–43, 47–48, 52, **53**, 67, 88

interest rates 6–7, 10–12, 14, 16, 25, 27, 52, 64, 70, 76, 79, 88, 97, 106, 142

International Islamic Fiqh Academy (IIFA) 130

International Monetary Fund (IMF) 33

Iran 127, 144–145, 147

Islam and finance: avoidance of *gharar* 5–6; concept of *riba* (interest) 4; nature and significance 3; risk-sharing 4–5; time value of money *5, 5*

Islam and financial risks: credit 98; diffusion 95–96; equity investment 101; fiduciary 98; firm's operations 101; foreign exchange risk 100–101; liquidity 99–100; management 96; market 97–98; rate of return 101; requirements 96; risk-sharing modes 94; risk types 97, *100*; Shari'ah noncompliance risk 98–99; theoretical positions on Islamic banking 93–94

Islam and governance: corporate governance 139–140; *Shari'ah* governance 140–142

Islamic banking: credit creation 10, 13–14, *14*; crisis on 31–32, *32*; development of 8; growth 21; installment financing 47; leverage control rate 11; in Muslim countries 22; Pakistan's contribution to 146; profit ratio in 11; rise of 8; sharing of investment risks 17–19

Islamic Banking Services Act in May 2013 127

Islamic bonds *see sukuk*

Islamic Development Bank (IDB) 78

Islamic economics 6, 21, 38, 107; system 107

Islamic finance: abolition 36; ban on interest 25–27; benevolent loan (*qard hasan*) 73–74; contracts 36, 47; determinants of ratios 35, 39–42, *40–41*; economic growth and development 29–31, 30; equity-based financing modes 36; factors and profit sharing 25–27; gold dinar 33–34; growth of assets 22, 24; instruments of *see* instruments; nominal-real circuitry 30; participatory modes of 38–42, 44; real economy 22, 24–25, 34; re-*takaful* in 121–122; sharing and investment 43–44; system convergence 31; The 2007 turmoil 31, *32*, 34, 129, 140

Islamic Finance Services Board (IFSB) 14, 130–131, 139, 141

Islamic financial institutions (IFIs) 142–143; dominance of diversity 125–126; need for regulations 129–130; perspective 124

Islamic financial instruments (IFIs) 99–100, 106

The Islamic Financial Services Board (IFSB) 14, 97, 99, 130–131, 139, 141; guidelines to manage risks 106–107

Islamic institutions 7, 36, 76, 99, 124, 128

Islamic insurance 114–115; beneficiary issue 113–114; business 112; concept 110, 122; contract 113; evolution 110–112; indemnity 113; insurable interest 112–113; proximate cause 113; *takaful vs.* insurance 115–116; uncertainty 122; underwriting 114; *see also takaful*

Islamic Malaysia Index 145

Islamic movement 148

ISRA Journal of Islamic Finance (2010) 47

istisna' 69, *69*, 73; *sukuk* 86–87, *86–87*

jualah 62

Juglar, Clément 24

Kamali, Hashim 36

Keynes, J. M. 6, 93

Knight, F. H. 92, 95

Kuala Lumpur 130, 145

law and Islamic finance: Basel Accords *see* Basel Accords; civil law 127; common law 126; IFIs 128; Islamic banking law 128; *Shari'ah* law 127

legal maxims 37–38

leverage control rate (LCR) 11, 15–17, 19

liability 17–18

liquidity 1–2, 8–9, 25, 56, 60, 62, 72–73, 75, 99–100, 107, 138

liquidity risk (LR) 62, 99–100, *100*, 107

London Interbank Offered Rate (LIBOR) 88, 97, 106

macroeconomics theory 93

Malaysia 27, 29, 33, 42, 48, 52, 57, 70–73, 78, 84, 88, 93–94, 99, 103, 127, 130, 132, 135, 145

Malaysian Southern Link Berhad (MSLB), 2008 87

Malik, Imam 66

marginal productivity theory 7, 26

market risk 97–98, *100*

Mecca 145

Mehta 28

Middle East and North Africa (MENA region) 146

MMP *vs.* ZDBM: comparative position **54**; ownership transfer 54–55, *55*, *55*; relative efficiency 55–57

Mohammad, Mahathir 33

money markets 60–61

monopoly theory 64

Morocco 147

mortgage 46, 48, 53–54, 57

mortgage-based loan contracts 47, 57

mudarabah 15–16, 18, 38, 94, 98; commodity 42; mixed system 39, *40*; and *musharakah* 38–39; participatory finance 141

mudarabah/musharakah 36, 44, 89

mudarabah sukuk (MS): capital 79; *mudarib* 79; Saudi 80; structural variations 80, *80*

murabahah 59, 97; AAOIFI 64; contracts 63; criticism 63–64; generic category of *uqud al-muawadhat* 62; markup issue 64–65; *Shari'ah* norms 63; *sukuk* 83–84, *84*

musharakah 25, 59; *Sharikat-ul-Milk* 65–66; *sukuk* 80–82, *81*

musharakah mutanaqisah 43

Musharka-Mutanaqisa Program (MMP) 47; BBA–sale with price deferment 52–53; compounding element in EMIs 50–52, *51*, **52**; diminishing balance 50; installment

payment 48–49; structure 47, 57, 63–64; violates Islamic law 58
Muslim: community 31, 147; countries 14, 22, 29, 33, 38, 60, 99, 127–130, 147; fertility rates in countries 22, 23; gold dinar as world currency 33–34; Indians 147; *vs.* world population growth **24**
muzaarah 36, 38, 44

The Nasir Social Bank 144
National Bank of Abu Dhabi 81
National *Shari'ah* Council of Malaysia 130
NCEIF 47
Nienhaus, Volker 130
non-investible businesses: infested with *gharar* (indeterminacy) 28; inviting unethical activities 28–29; involving speculation (maisir) 27–28

Office of Currency Comptroller (OCC) 132
operational risk (OR) *100*, 101
Organisation for Economic Co-operation and Development (OECD) 141, 143
ownership 46–47

pagan-era coins 33
Pakistan 29, 49, 67, 88, 127, 146–147
participatory finance 18, 25–26, 35, 38, 41, 90, 140–142
participatory modes 36, 38–42, 44
price: capital of *salam* 67–68; changes 12; index 11; level of 20
pricing 3, 47, 64, 73, 120–121, 123
profit-and-loss-sharing (PLS) 38–39, 82
profit-sharing ratios (PSRs) 15, *15*, 16, 38, 44, 79; determination 39–42, *40–41*

qard hasan 73–74, 98, 116, 144
Qatar 78
Qur'an 18, 29, 68, 125

rate of return (RRR) risk *100*, 101
RBI 50
real economy 22, 24–25, 34
Rehmatullah 148
reputation risk (RR) 100, *100*
Reserve Ratio (RR) 14
re-*takaful* company 121–122
riba-al-fadl 6

riba-al-nasiah 6
risk aversion 92, 93
risk management: dilemma of 91; IFSB guidelines 106–107; requirements 96; risk aversion 92; theory and practice of 91–92

saad-al-dharai 63
sakk see Sukuk
salam 67–68, 73; parallel *68*, 68–69; *sukuk* 84–86, *85*
secular law 125, 127–128
Shafi, Imam 64, 66
Shamil Bank of Bahrain 80
Shari'ah 25, 27, 70, 108; compliant 30, 43, 46, 48, 57, 79, 88, 102, 107, 116, 118, 147; frameworks *see* Shari'ah-based framework; governance 140–142; law 127; *maqasid* (goals) of 36; noncompliance risk 90, 98–99; norms 31, 57, 63, 88, 106, 120, 133, 145; objectives 96, 112, 114–115; requirements 22, 42, 76, 85; rules 80
The Shari'ah Advisory Council 122
Shari'ah-based framework: IFIs 130–132; legislation of Malaysia 132–133; regulatory issues 133; screening *see* Shari'ah screening
Shari'ah noncompliance risk (SCR) 98–99, 102, 107–108
Shari'ah screening 133–134; capital adequacy 134–135; on-and off-balance-sheet items 135; risk-weighted approach 136
Sitara Chemical Industries Ltd, 2002 82
socially responsible investing (SRI) 29
Standard Chartered Bank 81
Sudan 85, 120, 122, 127
sukuk 43; benchmarking 88–89; bonds, equity shares and 77–79; certificates 77–78; differences 76–77; *ijara* 82–83, *83*; investment 77; issuance 78; *istisna'* 86–87, *86–87*; market 88; meaning and origin 75–76; *mudarabah* 79–80, *80*; *murabahah* 83–84, *84*; *musharakah* 80–82, *81*; *salam* 84–86, *85*; securities 76; structuring 79

tabarru 117
Tabung Haji 145
takaful: cooperatives 119–120; forms of 116–117; *vs.* insurance 115–116;

156 Index

mudarabah model 117–118, *118*;
re-*takaful* 121–122; *waqf* model
118–119, *119*, 123; *see also* Islamic
insurance
tawarruq 71–72, *72*, 73, 88, 133
term finance certificates (TFCs) 82
trade cycle: phases 12, *12*; real and
money flows 12, *13*
trade-off 91–92
Turkey 25, 27, 88, 127–128
The 2007 financial crisis 31, *32*

UBS 81
Umar 44
Umar bin Al-khattab 114
United Arab Emirates 81, 87
US Federal Reserve Bank, 2013 138

Usmani, Sheikh Taqi 88

value of money 11–12, 20

wakala 43, 110, 118–119, 123
waqf 43, 113, 117; *takaful* 118–119,
119
Wealth of Nations 19
World Bank 33

Yemen 147

Zia-ul-Haq 146
Zubair Diminishing Balance Model
(ZDBM) 47; constructive ownership
53; diminishing balance model 53;
vs. MMP 54; structure *54*